African American Men and
Opportunity in the Navy

African American Men and Opportunity in the Navy

Personal Histories of Eight Chiefs

ARTHUR L. DUNKLIN

McFarland & Company, Inc., Publishers
Jefferson, North Carolina, and London

To the memory of
Mrs. Maggie Grandison and
Mr. Love Lee Grandison

LIBRARY OF CONGRESS CATALOGUING-IN-PUBLICATION DATA

Dunklin, Arthur L., 1967–
 African American men and opportunity in the Navy /
personal histories of eight chiefs / Arthur L. Dunklin.
  p.   cm.
 Includes bibliographical references and index.

 ISBN 978-0-7864-3699-6
 softcover : 50# alkaline paper ∞

 1. United States. Navy — African Americans. 2. United
States. Navy — Officers — Biography. I. Title.
VB324.A47D86   2008
359.0092'396073 — dc22   2008010221

British Library cataloguing data are available

©2008 Arthur L. Dunklin. All rights reserved

*No part of this book may be reproduced or transmitted in any form
or by any means, electronic or mechanical, including photocopying
or recording, or by any information storage and retrieval system,
without permission in writing from the publisher.*

On the cover: Saluting Chief ©2008 photoobjects.net; U.S.
Navy flag ©2008 Shutterstock

Manufactured in the United States of America

McFarland & Company, Inc., Publishers
 Box 611, Jefferson, North Carolina 28640
 www.mcfarlandpub.com

Table of Contents

Preface   1

Introduction   3

1. Equal Opportunity and Meritocracy
   in Practice: Inclusion or Exclusion   7
   - *Claims of Meritocracy in the U.S. Military*   7
   - *Meritocracy in the U.S. Navy: Principles and Stated Policies*   10
   - *Coping in Organizations of, by, and for Others*   16
   - *Summary*   19

2. Life and Career in the U.S. Navy   20
   - *Military Training*   21
   - *The Promotion Process*   22
   - *Mentorship*   25

3. Participants' Profiles   28
   - *Chief Andrews*   29
   - *Chief Butler*   35
   - *Chief Carter*   48
   - *Senior Chief Evanston*   54
   - *Senior Chief Gregg*   61
   - *Chief Hines*   71

Master Chief Ivans   81
Master Chief James   94

4. Barriers to Full Inclusion   108
   The Good Ol' Boys' Network   109
   The In-Group: A View from the Outside   111
   The Exceptional Negro   115
   Questioning Competence   116
   Affirmative Action: Misperceptions of "Reverse Discrimination"   118
   Limited Black Role Models   120

5. Mentorship   123
   The Navy's Formal Mentorship Program   124
   Informal Mentorship   127

6. Meritocracy or Myth of Meritocracy?   130

7. Resilience: How They Coped   139
   Overachieving   142
   Adaptation   143
   Minimization   145
   Self-Definition   147

8. Profiles in Struggle and Service   152
   Competence Questioned   153
   In-Group/Out-Group   154
   Limited Role Models   156
   But They Coped   157
   Negative Feelings   160

9. Implications for Navy Policies: A Prescription for Change   161
   Reassess the Current State   162
   Leadership Top-Down: Create an Equal Opportunity Climate   164

Revise the Current Evaluation System   165
Eliminate the "Just Like Me" Factor   165
Conclusion   166

References   169
Index   175

Preface

Few, if any, scholars argue that the society in which we live is a true meritocracy. To do so would beg the question, "Why do we need Title VII or the administrative agencies that enforce the equal opportunity policies of the federal and state governments?" If a nation has created a meritocracy, it would necessary follow that in times of budgetary constraints, there would be no need for the expenditure of taxpayer dollars to fund organizations that enforce unnecessary laws and policies.

Unlike the larger society, the military claims it has created an organization where merit is the sole determiner of one's potential level of success. Military leaders argue, and society generally accepts, the premise that one's race or sex does not serve as a barrier to achievement. My research in this area was designed to offer African American men an opportunity to paint a portrait of their existence within this military structure that purports to be free of racial bias. The study directly targets the U.S. Navy's claim of meritocracy and offers the reader an alternative view to that presented by the military's top leadership. The military, through its policies and ability to impose its will on its service members, has made great strides toward eliminating inequities. However, as a subset of the larger society, it is not immune to discrimination nor are its service members out of reach of discrimination's impact.

The military's bold claims of meritocracy are not without consequences. As with the larger society, the military can ill afford the expenditure of limited resources toward nonexistent problems. Thus, a likely outcome of an ill-conceived claim of meritocracy is a reduction of effort toward the elimination of inequality. The Navy is already showing signs of retreat. During the 1990s the military demonstrated its commitment to equal opportunity by investing significant resources toward training its workforce on issues of equality. However, in recent years, the military has made dramatic reductions in expenditures in its Equal Opportunity Management Institute, the Department of Defense's premier equal opportunity training facility.

Even in areas where there are no significant expenditures, the Navy is showing signs of retreat from its equal opportunity efforts. During previous iterations of the Navy's equal opportunity policy, commanders were instructed to write a local policy declaring their commitment to equal opportunity to help set the tone for those sailors under their command. The Navy's current policy has no requirement and, in the absence of this requirement, many commanders decline to issue their own policies. The elimination of such an inexpensive means of contributing to an equal opportunity climate is indicative of an organization that has become complacent in its efforts.

While the military is resting on its equal opportunity laurels, the statistics cited in society as signs of inequality appear as mirror images in the military. From advancement statistics to discipline rates and from feelings of inequality to disparities in training, African American servicemen fare worse than their White counterparts. Yet, in the face of these statistics, the military makes sweeping claims of meritocracy.

Further, the military's meritocracy claims, when viewed against the backdrop of the statistical data, raise additional questions that require answers. If the military is truly a meritocracy, why do African American men fare worse in almost all aspects of military life than do their White counterparts? The social implications of this are quite significant.

This work offers the military an opportunity to take another look at itself and to rethink its bold and sweeping assertion that it has done what no other organization of its size has ever done — eliminate inequality.

Introduction

In his description of African American men, Ellis Cose (2002) suggested, "Many of us are lost in this America of the twenty-first century. We are less sure of our place in the world than our predecessors, in part because our options, our potential choices, are so much grander than theirs. So we are trapped in a paradox" (p. 11). This paradox about which Cose speaks undoubtedly refers to the relative position of African American men in light of the absence of many of the overt legal barriers that have historically served to significantly limit their upward mobility. From employment levels to educational attainment and from discipline rates to healthcare statistics, African American men fail to reap the benefits of a prosperous society at levels equal to their White male counterparts.

Many of these men look to the military as a means of achieving higher levels of success. The military touts its success in creating a meritocracy within a society where merit is often sidelined by prejudice and discrimination. However, the literature on achievement and discipline statistics within the military closely mirrors that of other organizations. In the Navy, for instance, African American men are more likely to be discharged with an unfavorable discharge characterization. "Other Than Honorable" discharge characterizations strip military personnel of all military benefits and the option of ever returning to any branch of the military service. As of the fourth quarter of fiscal year 2005, African Americans, comprising 24.21 percent of those discharged, represented 30.72 percent of those receiving "Other Than Honorable" classifications. Comparatively, Whites, who represented 61.60 percent of those discharged, represented 58.82 percent of those receiving "Other Than Honorable" discharges (U.S. Navy, 2005).

Similar statistics exist for those who were subjected to judicial punishment. Judicial punishment, or court martial, is the military's equivalent of a trial by judge or judge and jury. Conviction at a court martial could leave the service member with a felony record that follows him or her into civilian life. During the fourth quarter of fiscal year 2005, African Americans represented 19.42 percent of the total enlisted force and represented 29.93 percent of those receiving judicial punishment. Whites, who comprised 66.54 percent of the enlisted force, comprised 58.82 percent of those who were referred for judicial punishment (U.S. Navy, 2005). Moreover, of the dozen military personnel on death row, nearly all are African American men (Hendren, 2006). The questions posed by such statistics, when those statistics are viewed against the backdrop of claims of meritocracy, have far-reaching implications.

Although the military suggests that merit determines a service member's levels of success, statistics from the U.S. Navy show that many significant disparities exist between African American males and White males in many areas, from promotion rates to incarceration rates and from discharge characterizations to their views on racial issues. For example, the demographic composition of the Navy at the end of the fourth quarter of fiscal year 2005 shows that African American men are consistently underrepresented in the most senior ranks when compared to their total representation in the force. In comparison, White men are consistently overrepresented in these ranks when compared to their total representation. Of the 214 admirals currently on active duty, 9 are African American males and none are African American females. Furthermore, as noted above, during the same period African Americans comprised 19.42 percent of the total enlisted force but represented 29.93 percent of those receiving judicial punishment. This is compared to Whites, who comprised 66.54 percent of the enlisted force and represented 58.82 percent of those receiving judicial punishment (U.S. Navy, 2005).

Similarly, sharp disparities exist between African American males and White males in the other branches of the military service. Fiscal year 2006 Coast Guard promotion rates reflect significant gaps in some areas between African Americans and Whites. For example, promotions to the rank of Lieutenant Commander reflect a 17 percent difference between African Americans and Whites, with African Americans promoting at a rate of 68 percent and Whites promoting at a rate of 85 percent (U.S. Coast Guard, 2005).

Although the Marine Corps suggests that its minority officer assessment conducted in 2004 shows the organization to be nondiscriminatory, its outcomes reflect large disparities that are similar to those cited by the other military branches. African Americans comprise significantly lower percentages of the officer corps than their representation in the service, comprising 11.9 percent of the total force and 5.6 percent of the officer corps. Comparatively, the representation of Whites among the officer corps exceeds their overall representation in the service, consisting of 64.3 percent of the total force and 77 percent of the officer corps (U.S. Marine Corps, 2005).

Thus, if one is to accept the assertion that the military is a meritocracy, where everyone, regardless of race, receives equal opportunities and attainment is based solely on merit, it would then also be necessary to offer another explanation for the disparity between Blacks and Whites in both attainment and discipline. Because of these far-reaching implications, there exists a need to subject these claims of meritocracy to rigorous scholarly scrutiny. However, the vast majority of the literature in this area tends to accept the assertion of a pure meritocracy without subjecting such claims to scrutiny.

Although the literature shows that there are differences between the attainment levels of African American men and White men in the military, as in many other areas of American life, many African American men do succeed within the military's system and achieve the highest enlisted ranks. What do they know about coping within the military's system that other African American men do not know? How have they managed to live and thrive in the military's hierarchical system that was built primarily to accommodate people from racial and cultural backgrounds other than their own? Moreover, are there lessons that they have learned through trials and struggles that can be helpful for other African American males who must also traverse a system that is often hostile to people from their racial and cultural backgrounds? The men in the study provide the reader a rare and candid look at the experiences of African American men in the United States Navy from their points of view. To protect them from possible retribution and to provide them the freedom to speak candidly, their names have been changed to protect their anonymity.

1

Equal Opportunity and Meritocracy in Practice: Inclusion or Exclusion

During specific periods in American history, events have "shocked" the nation and caused America to reexamine the role race plays in the nation's life and how inequalities are manifested based on race. Images, such as those that surfaced during the civil rights struggles of the 1950s and 1960s and those that surfaced more recently during the hurricane disaster in the U.S. Gulf Coast, have led to a short-lived public outcry regarding the state of racial inequality in the United States. Many organizations, both public and private, have for different reasons engaged in actions which they say are designed to remove barriers that are based on race. While many organizations have articulated desires for more diversity, and indeed many have instituted diversity programs, most show little progress in creating organizations where African American men are included in those positions of higher power and prestige. These men still struggle to be included in the boardrooms where major decisions are being made. Because of its claims of having created a more equitable work environment, many look to the Navy and the other branches of the military for an opportunity to compete on a more equal basis.

Claims of Meritocracy in the U.S. Military

A painting of the Battle of Bunker Hill produced in 1786 showed a Black soldier standing with a group of White rebel soldiers. However, reproductions of that painting produced some 20 years later reflect only the White soldiers. There was no mention of the Black soldier (Buckley, 2002). This scenario from the Revolutionary War vividly depicts the relationship Black military men have historically maintained with their country. Although much has changed with regard to race and racial segregation, the military has yet to achieve the meritocracy that is so often used as its descriptor.

Even as the military and many scholars suggest that the military has accomplished that which civilian sector organizations have been unable to — the creation of a meritocracy — the data provides a different view of the military. In 1996 and 1997, the Department of Defense administered the military-wide Equal Opportunity Survey (EOS). This was the first time the Defense Department had administered a survey of that magnitude (Scarville, Scott, Edwards, Lancaster & Elig, 1999) and it is the most current military-wide survey of the services' equal opportunity climate. The results of the survey were released in 1999 and provide a view of the military that is inconsistent with the view that the military has managed to carve out a segment of American society where merit alone is the determinant of success.

As in society in general, African Americans had a different perception of equal opportunity in the military than did Whites. For example, when asked if they were likely to be treated as "trouble" when members of their racial group congregated in groups, African Americans were nearly three times as likely as Whites to say they would be treated as trouble. While 12 percent of Whites responded that they would be treated as trouble when congregating with members of their own race, 35 percent of African Americans responded in the affirmative. Likewise, when asked if they had tried to avoid certain assignments because they thought they might be subjected to racial/ethnic harassment or discrimination, 98 percent of Whites and 93 percent of the Hispanic respondents stated they had not tried to avoid assignments for that reason. However, only 85 percent of African Americans responded in the same way — 13 percent fewer than Whites (Scarville, et al., 1999).

The disparity in responses existed in many of the areas tested. When asked to what extent they felt free to use military facilities, such as the dining halls and recreation facilities, regardless of their race or ethnicity, again, Whites were more likely to respond that they felt comfortable using these facilities than were their African American colleagues. When asked if they had experienced a racial confrontation on a military installation or ship, there existed a 17 percentage point difference between African American respondents and White respondents, with African Americans being significantly more likely to report having experienced a racial confrontation on the installation or ship (Scarville, et al., 1999).

However, even with the disparities between the perceptions of Whites and African Americans, overall, all groups reported that the racial climate in the military is better than that outside the services. Additionally, all groups reported having at least as many friends who are of a different race or ethnicity as they had before entering the service. When asked about their prospects for promotion, African Americans were more likely than Whites to say the opportunities were either better or no different than in the civilian sector. However, when asked if they felt they would receive the assignments they needed for promotions, Whites were more likely than African Americans to say they would receive the assignments that would help them achieve promotions (Scarville, et al., 1999).

While the EOS measured the perceptions of the military members, the actual outcomes, in terms of promotions, reveal stark differences between the actual opportunities for African Americans and Whites in the military. In the Army, for instance, in 1998 African Americans accounted for 26.6 percent of the Army and 11.1 percent of the officer corps. However, as one looks higher in the officer ranks, there is a noticeable disparity between the representation of African Americans in the lower ranks and those in the higher ranks. In 1998, up to the rank of Major (O-4), African Americans accounted for about 12 percent of the officer corps. However, in the higher ranks, the percentage decreases by nearly 50 percent, while the percentage of White officers enjoys a 10 percent increase (Butler, 1999).

Similarly, promotion rates in the Coast Guard reflect a sharp disparity between the advancement rates of White officers and African American officers. Fiscal year 2006 Coast Guard promotions to the rank of Lieutenant Commander (O-4) show a 17 percent difference between the promotion rates of African Americans and Whites, with African Americans promoting at a rate of 68 percent, and Whites promoting at a rate of 85 percent (U.S. Coast Guard, 2005). The Marine Corps 2005 Force Management Oversight Council's 2005 brief asserted "Minority officer assessment conducted in 2004 indicates the Marine Corps to be a non-discriminatory organization" (p. 3). However, while African Americans and Whites made up 11.9 percent and 63.3 percent of the Marine Corps, respectively, there was a significantly larger gap between the percentage of African American and White officers. Although they made up 11.9 percent of the total force, African Americans made up only 5.6 percent of the officer corps, a significantly lower percentage. Alternatively, while Whites made up 64.3 percent of the total force, they accounted for 77 percent of the total officer corps, a correspondingly higher percentage (U.S. Marine Corps, 2005).

While the military, like society in general, has made progress in improving the opportunities for African Americans, the data do not seem to support claims that the services have created a meritocracy. The literature shows that many of the same issues faced by African American men and other minority groups in the larger society exist within the military services.

Meritocracy in the U.S. Navy: Principles and Stated Policies

It was primarily the events within the Navy that ushered in a new focus on working toward a more equal environment within the military services. The U.S. Navy's recent history caused it to pause and examine the role race plays in the way the organization functions. The service was prodded, not merely by acts of conscience and the belief in the innate right to equality of opportunities, but by events that threatened to reduce the organization's capacity to carry out its function.

In July of 1972, while the United States was engaged in the Vietnam War, the availability of two aircraft carriers was called into question due to problems brought on by racial strife among their crews. In the first incident, African American men, who perceived that they were the victims of racial discrimination, gathered as a group to present their grievances to the ship's commanding officer. Among their grievances were complaints that African American sailors were subjected to non-judicial punishment at significantly higher rates than Whites were and that they comprised a much higher rate of administrative separations than Whites did. They demanded a review of the ship's non-judicial punishment and administrative separation records to determine if the commanding officer had discriminated against African American sailors (U.S. Congress, 1973).

Later, in October of that same year, a similar incident happened onboard the aircraft carrier USS *Kitty Hawk* while it was preparing to return to combat in Southeast Asia. During this incident, however, there were actual physical conflicts throughout the ship between Black sailors and White sailors. Using the ship's damage control devices — dogging wrenches, metal pipes, and fire extinguisher nozzles — the sailors engaged in armed conflict against each other along racial lines for more than 7 hours (U.S. Congress, 1973).

Although the Congressional report stated that it found no substantial evidence of racial discrimination, it stated that many perceptions of discrimination existed among African American sailors (U.S. Congress, 1973). As a result of these events, the Navy — perhaps more than the other services — articulated a true and hard-learned understanding of the importance of ensuring equal opportunities for its sailors without regard for their race. This newfound understanding led to the development of policies and procedures that were designed to promote equal opportunities for the services' racial and ethnic minorities. Additionally, the Department of Defense commissioned a task force headed by Major General Lucius Theus to examine the causes and find possible solutions for racial strife within the Navy and other services. One outcome of this commission was the establishment of the Defense Race Relations Institute, which later became the Defense Equal Opportunity Management Institute. The institute's original charge was to train members of all services to return to their respective units and serve as equal opportunity representatives and to provide equal opportunity training for others in their organizations (Calkins, 2004).

However, in recent years, many view the military as a true meritocracy where merit alone determines one's level of achievement (Quester & Gilroy, 2002). The result of such assertions could lead to complacency and a retreat from efforts designed to root out discrimination and the effects years of unequal treatment have caused for African Americans and other minorities within the military services. The Navy already shows signs of retreat. Whereas in previous years the Department of the Navy mandated specific methods for assessing equal opportunity climates in the various individual units within the naval services, the current policies allow individual units to conduct these assessments using any methods they deem appropriate, not excluding those methods that have not been tested to ensure reliability and validity and those that have been shown to be ineffective (CNO, 1999). Additionally, whereas in past years the Navy required commanding officers to issue written personal statements to those under their supervision outlining the commander's personal commitment to equal opportunity and mandating that all levels of the chain of command adopt an equal commitment, the most recent Navy policy on equal opportunity has no such requirement (U.S. Navy, 2001). The literature on organizational culture stresses the importance of leaders' setting and reinforcing important aspects of organizational culture (Schneider, 1997) and such a change may signal a change in course for efforts to promote equal opportunity.

While many assert that the Navy has achieved a meritocracy, as with the other services, the data present a different picture. As late as 1997, the literature indicated that institutional racism, human capital shortages, and inaccessibility to informal White male networks cause African American men and other minorities to promote at lower rates than White males do (Baldwin, 1997). Further, among officer and enlisted ranks, the demographic composition of the Navy at the end of the fourth quarter of fiscal year 2005 shows that African Americans are consistently underrepresented in the most senior ranks when compared to their total representation in the force. In comparison, Whites are consistently overrepresented in these ranks when compared to their total representation. Furthermore, during the same period, while African Americans comprised 19.42 percent of the total enlisted force, they represented 29.93 percent of those receiving judicial punishment. This is compared to Whites, who comprised 66.54 percent of the enlisted force and represented 58.82 percent of those receiving judicial punishment (U.S. Navy, 2001).

An even greater disparity exists among those who receive discharges categorized as "Other Than Honorable," which strips them of any military benefits and the option of ever returning to any branch of the military. African Americans, comprising 24.31 percent of those discharged, represented 30.72 percent of those receiving the "Other Than Honorable" classification. At the same time, Whites, comprising 61.60 percent of those leaving the Navy, represented 58.82 percent of those receiving the "Other Than Honorable" classification (U.S. Navy, 2005). Additionally, in the most recent Navy Equal Opportunity and Sexual Harassment (NEOSH) Survey taken in 1999 and 2000, the data revealed that, as in society at large, Blacks and Whites have significantly different perceptions about the existence of discrimination (U.S. Navy, 2001).

In spite of the challenges African Americans face in their struggle to achieve within the military, many have succeeded. Many African Americans — including African American females — have made slow but significant progress within the naval service. It was not until 1980 that Ensign Brenda Robinson became the Navy's first African American female aviator (Hodge, 1995), and today the Navy has three African American female pilots on active duty. However, a review of the Navy's demographic data reveals a decreasing representation of African American men and women in the higher levels of the rank structure. Of the 214 admirals currently on active duty, 9 are African American males and none are African American females. African American men and women fare better among the ranks of other senior Navy officers. For example, there are 100 African American men and 21 African American women serving in the rank of Navy captain (O-6). Additionally, among the enlisted ranks, there are 26 African American females serving in the most senior enlisted rank (Master Chief) and 314 African American men (U.S. Navy, 2006).

While the progress being made by African American women is important to the overall view of African American progress in the Navy, this study focuses exclusively on African American males' struggles to achieve because the Navy has, until very recently, greatly restricted the positions available to all females. Moreover, some designators under special warfare and submarine warfare remain closed to women (U.S. Navy, 2006). Also, African American males have historically served, and continue to serve, a critical function within the Black family, both as role models for young African American males and as the primary source of financial stability for many families.

The discussion in this chapter highlights many disparities between the achievement levels of African American men and White men. In many different segments of American life, from leadership roles in sports to the corporate boardroom to the military, disparities exist between the achievement levels of African American men and their White male counterparts. However, many of the same disparities exist among other marginalized groups in American society. The literature indicates that women continue to strive to achieve parity with men in almost all areas of corporate life. A 2000 study by Kevin Hallock at the University of Illinois indicated that top female executives at America's largest companies are paid significantly less, on average — approximately 45 percent less — than males in similar positions. A large portion of the disparity in earnings between women executives and men executives can be accounted for by the fact that women

Figure 1. Promotion Requirements

Pay grade	Standard Score (SS)			Performance			FACTORS Service in Pay Grade (SIPG)			Awards			Pass Not Advanced (PNA)			Maximum Final Multiple Score Possible (100%)
	computation	points		computation	points		computation	points		computation	points		computation	points		
E-4/E-5	indicated on exam profile sheet	80 (34%)		(PMA* × 60)–156	84 (36%)		(2 × SIPG) +15	30 (13%)		varies based on award	10 (4%)		2 × PNA points from last 5 exam cycles	30 (13%)		234
E-6	indicated on exam profile sheet	80 (30%)		(PMA* × 60)–130	110 (41.5%)		(2 × SIPG) +19	34 (13%)		varies based on award	12 (4.5%)		2 × PNA points from last 5 exam cycles	30 (11%)		266
E-7	indicated on exam profile sheet	80 (60%)		PMA* × 13	52 (40%)											132

*Performance Mark Average (PMA) is determined based on performance evaluation rating
(Source: Advancement Manual for the Advancement of Enlisted Personnel of U.S. Navy and U.S Naval Reserve, July 25, 2001)

are much less likely to be the chair or chief executive of the company. The highest percentage of female executives existed in the ranks of senior vice president (3.5 percent of the total), chief financial officer (6.4 percent), and executive vice president (2.7 percent). However, only .52 percent of all CEOs and chairs of the board of the 1,500 companies in the study were women (Reutter, 2000).

Like African Americans and women, Hispanics are greatly underrepresented among those in America's corporate boardrooms. In her February 2004 remarks before the Hispanic Association on Corporate Responsibility, Ingrid Duran, president and CEO of the Congressional Hispanic Caucus Institute, reported that just 1.97 percent of Fortune 1000 corporate board seats are held by Hispanics. She further added that, of those, Hispanic women hold only 34 out of 10,314 seats. The literature indicates that among the important factors affecting the success of Hispanics is discrimination and the availability and quality of mentors. Similar factors have been cited as factors affecting the success of African American men (Duran, 2004).

However, some African American males have managed to reach the highest levels of their profession. In the area of sports, while the numbers are few, African American males have achieved the level of head coach. In corporate America, some have ascended the corporate structure to serve at the top of companies like American Express. In the Navy, although in disproportionately low numbers, they have risen to the highest levels. Unlike many workplaces in the United States, the Navy has articulated in its policies what it says are the objective standards by which promotion decisions are made.

The Advancement Manual for the Advancement of Enlisted Personnel of U.S. Navy and U.S. Naval Reserve explicates what the Navy says are its objective requirements for promotion through the enlisted advancement system. Promotions to pay grades E-1 and E-2 are automatically entered once the service person has served 9 months as an E-1 or E-2. Although these promotions are automatically entered without any examination or other action, the sailor's commanding officer (CO) may delay these promotions if he or she deems it appropriate. To do so, the CO must submit necessary documents to Navy Personnel Command informing them that the service member's promotion is to be delayed (BUPERSINST 1430.16E, 2001). Although the CO is the authorizing official for delaying promotions to E-2 and E-3, the process is initiated at levels far below the level of commanding officer.

Promotions to the higher enlisted levels have significantly more requirements. Factors such as the service member's score on a standardized advancement examination, performance evaluations, amount of time in the current pay grade, awards, and points earned from passing previous examinations at levels not high enough for promotion (PNA points) are combined to determine whether the sailor is promoted to the next rank. The weight assigned to each of these factors changes as the individual competes for higher ranks. Figure 1 below depicts the requirements at the different levels up to the rank of E-7 (Chief).

Promotions to the ranks of Chief (E-7), Senior Chief (E-8), and Master Chief (E-9) require action by a selection board. Candidates competing for E-7 who are determined selection board eligible by competing in a Navy-wide examination and meeting the minimum final multiple for their rating must have their records reviewed by a selection board convened annually by the Chief of Naval Personnel. Candidates competing for E-8 and E-9 are designated selection board eligible on the basis of their Commanding Officer's recommendation (BUPERSINST 1430.16E, 2001). This process, although presented as objective, contains many areas where subjective appraisals are used to determine promotion opportunities. Further, while the literature on the Navy's enlisted advancement system details the promotion rates of African American men, other minorities, and women in comparison to Whites and men, the Navy has not commissioned a study to determine the role race plays in its advancement process. In spite of the potential for subjectively made decisions, many African American men do succeed within this system. If it is possible for these men to succeed, why can't others? What information can these achievers pass on to others who must work their way through organizational structures that were not designed by or for them? What coping mechanisms do they employ?

Coping in Organizations of, by, and for Others

Morgan (1997), in his discussion of organizations as psychic prisons, asserts that much of what goes on within organizations occurs below the level of the human conscious and that in understanding organizational structures one must consider the hidden structure and dynamics of the human psyche. This view suggests that the constructs of organizations are, to a large extent, the manifestation of the human subconscious. Thus, organizations are very much a part of those who construct them, and those who would successfully fit must do so in a manner that is compatible with the culture that has been established. Often, the manifestations of these cultures do not consider the life experiences of those African American men who must work within them.

On a societal level, W.E.B. DuBois discussed how African Americans live a dual existence in order to fit the expectations of the dominant group while retaining their own cultural attributes (Du Bois, 1903, 1989). Similarly, most organizations in the United States — both public and private — were established by White men and the norms and expectations were set by members of this group. The literature shows that those who are not members of this group use many different means of coping as outsiders within organizations that were not created by or for them.

Predominantly White workplaces seldom accommodate interests and values that are associated with African Americans. Rather, Blacks are expected to assimilate to the norms of those in the majority. In order to rise within these organizations, some African American executives conclude that they must choose between their own Black identity and corporate enculturation (Cose, 2002). Because they find this choice untenable, many African Americans in senior positions within organizations often find themselves resisting pressures to think or become White (Feagin & Sikes, 1994). Others submit to these pressures and, as Ella Bell revealed in her 1990 study of African American professionals and managers, find themselves being considered as different from other Blacks. One of Bell's respondents stated:

> The temptation is that we begin to think that we are an exception to other black folks. And most of the time when we step out on that, we get burned, because we would become coopted into the white community, into the white value system, and to the white frame of thinking. We excise ourselves from the black community, or we stay with our Afro-Americanness and take the risk of offending our white friends [Bell, 1990, p. 475].

While some African Americans cope by attempting to assimilate to the norms of Whites within their organizations, others cope by lowering their expectations for achievement. Feagin and Sikes (1994) suggest that some organizations engage in a process of social cloning whereby they attempt to groom upwardly mobile employees to act in a way that is comfortable for the majority. Some African Americans, who believe they will never be able to fit within that socially acceptable group, accept that Whites will always have the advantage and minimize their expectation for their own achievement. As described by Mirowsky and Ross (1989), one's minority status is associated "with a reduced sense of control ... partly because for members of minority groups, any given level of achievement requires greater effort and provides fewer opportunities" (p.16). Rather than endure the stress, many lower their expectations.

However, the literature indicates that those African Americans existing within the middle class often exist within a minority culture of mobility (Neckerman, Carter & Lee, 1999). This culture serves as a means by which they may cope with the stresses of daily existence within predominantly White organizations. Within this culture, African American political organizations, formal and informal networks, and groups are established that provide support and information on how to present oneself to Whites. This culture serves as a refuge and a space within which they may debrief from their day of movement within predominantly White organizations (Cole & Omari, 2003). It also instills the importance of behaviors and consumption that is appropriate for their class (Lee, 2000). Although they exist on a different stratum within the economic order, they are often not much better off than Blacks in the working class (Collins, 1983). This is true, in part, because (unlike Whites existing within the same economic stratum) most middle-class African Americans did not inherit their status. As a result there is little guarantee that their upward mobility will be sustained (Vanneman & Cannon, 1987).

Whereas anger and rage are often outcomes of African American men working or traversing historically White workplaces, these coping mechanisms serve as a means of subduing their passions. However, Dr. Price Cobbs (2005) suggests that many African Americans do not have positive outlets for this rage that results from their experiences within the workplace. If they cannot avoid the situation that is causing the stress, they may withdraw socially or avoid comparison with the nonstigmatized group (Crocker & Major, 1989). Although such social avoidance may relieve the stress that accompanies acknowledging how others benefit at their expense, this type of withdrawal does not prove to be particularly beneficial over the long term, as exclusive comparison with other African Americans does not lead to positive change (Miller & Kaiser, 2001).

Minimization is another type of disengagement mechanism that African American men may use. By minimizing, the individual avoids the stress by denying the existence of discrimination even when the facts indicate discrimination has occurred. Additionally, discrimination creates vulnerability within African American men because they are robbed of a sense that they have control and that they can be accepted by others (Ruggiero, Taylor & Lydon, 1997). As with social avoidance, the literature shows that minimization has a poor track record and may lead to physical symptoms, maladjustment and psychological stress (Major, Richards, Cooper, Cozzarelli & Zubek, 1998; Holohan, Moos & Schaefer, 1996).

Summary

As the literature suggests, many African Americans have managed to cope and to succeed within organizations that are often hostile to them. However, many others have not. Within the military, there exists a significant disparity between the rate of success achieved by White men and African American men. Further, African American men are more likely to be represented among those who receive judicial and non-judicial punishment, more likely to receive negative discharge characterizations (some of which may impact them even as they return to civilian life), and more likely to be represented among those on the military's death row. As a microcosm of the military, the Navy has taken specific steps, prompted by hard-learned lessons, that it says were designed to create equal opportunities for all racial groups. However significant disparities remain.

Even in light of these disparities many suggest that the military services have created a meritocracy, where all are free to achieve as far as their abilities will allow. Such an assertion has significant and far-reaching implications. Thus, it is necessary to understand how those who have managed to succeed successfully navigated the Navy's hierarchical system. A determination of the strategies they employed and their views of the military's claim of meritocracy may be useful for both the military and those African American men who have yet to succeed in the Navy's system.

2

Life and Career in the U.S. Navy

Though they each have different functions and perform different roles as instruments of power projection and national defense, there are many commonalities among the different branches of the U.S. military. Each, using its own methods, seeks to transform civilian men and women into military personnel who willingly abide by a general code of behavior that is uniquely military and which serves as a minimum requirement for military life. A critical component of this military code is the willingness to submit to the authority of those appointed over them. So critical is this component that it is an important part of the oath that is required of all enlisted personnel. All enlistees in each branch of the military services are bound by the following oath of enlistment:

> I, (state your name), do solemnly swear (or affirm) that I will support and defend the Constitution of the United States against all enemies, foreign and domestic; that I will bear true faith and allegiance to the same; and that I will obey the orders of the President of the United States and the orders of the officers appointed over me, according to regulations and the Uniform Code of Military Justice. So help me God.

Also implicit in this oath, and made explicit in the Uniform Code of Military Justice, United States Naval Regulations, and other military regulations, is the requirement to respect those who are senior in rank and position. Perhaps more than any other organization in American life, the military emphasizes this respect for rank and position, stating that "Any warrant officer or enlisted member who treats with contempt or is disrespectful in language or deportment toward a warrant officer, non-commissioned officer, or petty officer while that officer is in the execution of his office; shall be punished as a court-martial may direct" (Uniform Code of Military Justice, 2006). In addition to policies and coercive measures that are designed to reinforce the military's emphasis on following orders, the military's training programs are another tool by which this expectation is transmitted and reinforced.

Military Training

This requirement and other basic requirements of military life serve as the foundation for each of the services' basic military training. While much of this training focuses on physical fitness and the technical requirements of the specific service, the pedagogical methods used have embedded within them behavioral conditioning that teaches the service members far more than the technical aspects of performing their jobs. It is during this training that the military begins to inculcate the ethos of sacrifice for one's fellow service members, the unit, the mission, and the country. Each service makes explicit its core values and defines those values in ways that support this ethos.

The Navy's basic training is an 8-week training program that takes place at Naval Training Center, Great Lakes, IL. During those 8 weeks of training, the Navy's core values of honor, courage, and commitment are explicitly discussed with the would-be sailors and inform the pedagogy used to transform individual citizens into sailors who, to a large extent, sacrifice their individualism for membership in a team. Further, those values are defined in ways that support the team concept, service to country, commitment to duty, selflessness, and fidelity. For its own purposes, the Navy defines honor as bearing true faith and allegiance. This concept is to be manifested in several outcomes: (a) ethical conduct, (b) honest and truthful dealing with colleagues, (c) making and receiving honest recommendations, (d) integrity and responsibility, (e) legal and ethical conduct in personal and professional lives, and (f) cognizance of the privilege to serve one's country.

Similarly, the Navy defines courage in a way that helps to transform the consciousness of those who join its ranks. For this purpose, courage is defined as the commitment to support and defend. Courage is to be manifested in the following outcomes: (a) meeting the demands of the military profession and the mission when it is hazardous, demanding or otherwise difficult; (b) adhering to higher standards of decency and conduct while meeting challenges; (c) placing the interests of the nation and the Navy above regard to personal consequences; (d) maintaining mental and moral strength to do that which is right in the face of adversity; and (e) maintaining loyalty to the nation by ensuring resources are used in a careful, efficient, and honest way.

The Navy's third core value — commitment — reinforces the importance of adhering to orders and demonstrating respect for the military chain of command. Commitment is defined as obeying orders. To live up to this core value, sailors are expected to manifest the following behaviors: (a) insisting on respect up and down the chain of command; (b) demonstrating concern for those they supervise; (c) treating others with dignity; (d) showing moral character, competence in one's profession, quality work, and technical excellence; (e) showing respect irrespective of one's religion, race, or sex; (f) demonstrating commitment to constant improvement and positive change; and (g) exhibiting a commitment to working together as a team for continuous improvement.

The Navy's training and core values place significant emphasis on devotion to duty and readiness to sacrifice for the team and for the mission. Its core values stress individual respect, human dignity, and commitment to the team. However, in spite of this, few African American men and women would deny that they have experienced the reality of racism and racially based discrimination. This dichotomy between the Navy's espoused values and the reality experienced by African Americans has created a sort of dual reality, whereby African Americans exist within the team but because of inequities — either actual or perceived — in promotions and other opportunities, they fail to be truly integrated within the team.

The Promotion Process

In the Navy, Chief Petty Officers, Senior Chief Petty Officers, and Master Chief Petty Officers are the senior enlisted managers. Residing in pay grades E-7 to E-9, they exercise significant authority in managing sailors in pay grades E-1 to E-6. Sailors in pay grades E-4 to E-6 are considered Petty Officers. The most junior enlisted sailors reside in pay grades E-1 to E-4.

2. Equal Opportunity and Meritocracy in Practice 23

The military services have detailed explanations of their promotion processes which they say reflect objective criteria for promotions. The Navy's enlisted promotion system is detailed in the *Advancement Manual for the Advancement of Enlisted Personnel of U.S. Navy and U.S. Naval Reserve* (Advancement Manual). Personnel in pay grades E-1 and E-2 are advanced at the commanding officer's discretion upon completion of required time in current grade. While personnel in pay grades E-3 to E-6 must compete for advancement through a written examination, those in pay grades E-7 to E-9 must be nominated by their commanding officers to compete for advancement. Once nominated, their selection for promotion is based on their prior performance as reflected in their military service record and no written examination is required. Selection boards make their determination based on service record items such as the nature and type of assignments completed, performance at those assignments (as reflected in the performance evaluation), enlisted qualifications earned, schools attended, awards earned, and rankings relative to one's peers (as reflected in the performance evaluations).

The Advancement Manual details the requirements for Navy personnel to advance from E-1 to E-9 and the conditions under which those promotions may be withheld or delayed. The Navy considers the commanding officer's recommendation to be the most important eligibility requirement for promotions. These recommendations are made as a part of the sailor's performance evaluation and the most recent performance evaluation is the only source of this recommendation. Although commanding officers may withhold a recommendation due to poor performance, they may not withhold these recommendations due to lack of observation. The Advancement Manual provides detailed guidance on the conditions under which a commanding officer may withhold recommendations for advancement and the requirements of withholding such recommendations (U.S. Navy, 2001).

In addition to the commanding officer's recommendation, Navy personnel must serve a minimum time in the current pay grade prior to promoting to the next level. To be eligible for promotion from E-3, personnel must remain 6 months at that grade. Personnel in pay grades E-1 and E-2 must remain in their current pay grade at least 9 months prior to promoting to the next level. Personnel in pay grade E-4 must remain in that grade for a minimum of 1 year prior to promoting to E-5. Promotions to E-6 through E-9 require personnel to remain in their current pay grade for at least 36 months. The Advancement Manual states the specific months by which the service member must have achieved the required time in pay grade in order to be eligible for promotion during any given cycle (U.S. Navy, 2001a).

Completion of appropriate service schools is another important requirement for promotions in certain enlisted professions. For example, the Advancement Manual requires that in order for personnel to be eligible to compete for promotion to Chief Meteorologist, they must meet all previously stated requirements and complete the Meteorological Oceanographic Analysis Forecaster Course. Similarly, prior to achieving eligibility to compete for promotion to Legalman Third Class, personnel must have successfully completed the Naval Justice School. The Navy's technical training requirements for different specialties vary and change from time to time. However, Navy training courses are an integral part of the promotion process and failure to complete certain Navy schools can disqualify individuals for promotions to pay grades as junior in rank as E-4. For example, in order to compete for promotion to E-6, E-7, or E-8, personnel must first complete the Navy's Leadership Training Continuum that is appropriate for their current pay grade. Waivers may be granted that permit individuals to compete without completing this training. However, such waivers must be requested at the level of the first admiral in the service member's chain of command. Because of the political implications of seeking waivers at such a high level, commanding officers are often reluctant to support such a request unless the mission or other uncontrollable circumstances prevented the service member from completing the course (U.S. Navy, 2001a).

Navy personnel must also receive a performance evaluation that was completed within the computation period for the appropriate advancement cycle in order to be eligible to compete for advancement. However, personnel in pay grades E-1 to E-9 who are otherwise qualified to compete for advancement will not be disqualified to compete due to special medical or disciplinary status. Navy personnel who are qualified to compete for promotion and who are hospitalized for reasons other than their own misconduct may still compete for advancement if the commanding officer of the Navy hospital determines them to be mentally and physically capable to compete. Similarly, those who are undergoing medical treatment or awaiting action by a clinical board, medical survey board, or physical evaluation board may compete for promotion if the ongoing treatment or pending medical board action is not the result of the individual's own misconduct that is subject to disciplinary action (U.S. Navy, 2001a).

The Navy's Advancement Manual provides detailed discussion of the requirements that must be met prior to achieving eligibility for competition at the various levels. That manual also details the conditions under which promotions may be denied or delayed. However, the manual does not address the human factor that may play a role in what the Advancement Manual considers to be one of the more important requirements — performance evaluations. While enlisted performance evaluations (for E-1 to E-6) and fitness reports (for E-7 to O-10) provide specific categories that must be evaluated, they remain quite subjective, leaving the evaluation to the discretion of the evaluator. Further, while the commanding officer is the final determiner of one's ranking among peers and the recommendation for advancement, he or she is typically far removed from the individual being evaluated. Thus, the recommendations provided to the commanding officer by lower level supervisors often determine evaluation outcomes. This, combined with the lack of a requirement for any documentation and the subjective nature of the evaluation process, leaves open the possibility of bias affecting the outcomes (U.S. Navy, 2001a).

Mentorship

Although the military services provide clear guidance on what they say are the objective requirements for promotion, mentorship is another factor to consider. In recent years the military has increasingly focused on the role of the mentor-protégé relationship in developing personnel to fulfill the services' many functions and in helping sailors advance their careers. The services have come to the conclusion that mentorship is crucial for professional growth and retention. Further, they argue that adequate mentorship reduces the likelihood that sailors will become disciplinary problems. As pointed out by the commanding officer of the Navy Space and Naval Warfare Systems Command (SPAWAR) in his September 2003 policy,

> Experience has shown the Navy, its commands and the individual, have reaped the benefits of mentorship since the birth of our service. It has also been demonstrated the best sailors were and are mentored by the best leaders. A sailor who receives proper attention, both professionally and personally, has more potential to realize personal goals and is more inclined to remain a sailor.

> Conversely, the sailor who does not realize their personal and professional goals, or who, for whatever reason, did not receive an adequate level of mentorship tends to be an administrative burden and ultimately decides to terminate their naval career. This leaves both the Navy and individual dissatisfied [Slaght, 2003, p. 1].

Because of their belief in the importance of mentorship to their missions, each military service has moved forward with incorporating its own formal mentorship programs. In his 2003 guidance for leaders, the Chief of Naval Operations stressed the importance of mentoring sailors and directed all Navy units to create a mentoring culture and assign a mentor for all Navy personnel by March 2003. As a result, different Navy organizations embarked upon designing programs to mentor their sailors. While different organizations approached this task differently, there are some characteristics that tend to be present in most Navy mentorship programs.

The written designation of a mentor is a frequent component of Navy mentor programs. This mentor may be selected by the protégé or, on some occasions, the mentor is designated by the service member's chain of command. The same mentors may be, and often are, assigned to more than one sailor. Some Navy organizations limit the number of protégés that a mentor may have, based on the seniority of the mentor and the rank of the protégé. For example, while those at all levels of the chain of command are typically required to have a mentor, because of their seniority, officers in pay grades O-4 and above and Chiefs are believed to require less frequent mentorship than are more junior officers and junior enlisted personnel. Thus, their mentors may be assigned several protégés (Slaght, 2003).

Another frequent component of Navy mentorship programs is placing responsibility for mentorship program management with the Chiefs within the command. Because of their experience and because the majority of personnel in most commands are supervised — either directly or indirectly — by Chiefs, Chiefs are generally held responsible for the success or failure of the Navy's mentorship programs. The commanding officer of SPAWAR asserts "the Chief has the requisite experience to recognize the needs of our junior sailors. I thereby hold them accountable for the success of this program" (Slaght, 2003, p. 4).

While in recent years the military has focused significant attention on formal mentorship programs, mentors are not new to the military. Informal mentors have always been around and have served an important role in providing advice and guidance to help develop junior service members. Many view these informal mentors to be more significant in their career development than formally appointed mentors. However, in many cases, informal mentors were selective in choosing protégés and groups that have been traditionally marginalized in the larger society were often deprived of the benefits of mentorship. The military's formal mentorship programs are designed to extend the benefits of the mentor-protégé relationship to all service members.

3

Participants' Profiles

The military, perhaps more than other organizations, through its well-defined and articulated rules, policies, and core values, provides a clear picture of the ideal sailor, marine, soldier, or airman. The expectations presented through those means are designed to provide a blueprint of what the military says is necessary to succeed within the respective service. Those who fill those ranks are derived from different backgrounds and enlist for different reasons. Their experiences within the services are often qualitatively different, with some finding it more difficult to fit within the organization's culture. Others fit well and thrive within the rigid military structure.

As with other senior enlisted Navy personnel, the African American men in this study came from different parts of the country and have served the Navy in different organizations. However, each has been immersed within the Navy's culture for a period that typically ranges from 10 to 30 years and has succeeded in joining the ranks of the most senior enlisted group — Chief, Senior Chief, or Master Chief. The quality of their self-reported experiences as they ascended through the ranks varies and each has articulated different means of coping within the Navy structure. In the following pages I introduce the participants in this study, profiling their subjective experiences and views of the Navy and how they say they coped. Through these introductions, the reader is provided a better sense of who the participants are and their views of the Navy. Pseudonyms are used to protect the identities of those Chiefs, Senior Chiefs, and Master Chiefs in the study.

Chief Andrews

Chief Andrews enlisted in the Navy right out of high school and was selected for Chief after 10½ years on active duty. Although he knew he would enlist in the military, the Navy was not necessarily preferred over any of the other branches of the armed forces. In fact, he stated that he was initially looking to join the Air Force but he could not locate an Air Force recruiter. He ended up joining the Navy because he came across a Navy recruiter first. He cites several reasons for joining the military. As with many who enlist, he cites economics as one reason for enlisting. He stated that he wanted to "make it a little easier financially" for his mother and brother and to change the environment in which he was living. He specifically stated, "I guess the main reason I joined the Navy [was to] see the world [and] all that jive that went with it also. It was mainly to ... get out of where I was living."

Although he knew he would join the military, Chief Andrews did not have intentions of staying in the Navy for an entire career. He stated that he intended to serve for a 4-year term and then leave the military and return to school. However, after he enlisted, he got married and started a family. He stated that it was primarily these changes that influenced him to stay in the Navy beyond his first enlistment. At this point, he had not considered how long he would stay or what his career aspirations were. He did, however, apply and was accepted for an officer commissioning program. He stated that he had to decline the commission due to his family obligations. Even at this point, he had not decided that he would definitely make the Navy a career. That decision, he said, came much later.

Under normal circumstances, the 20-year mark is the earliest a sailor may enter into a type of retirement known as "fleet reserve." Entering into the fleet reserve means that the sailor has earned all the rights and privileges of a full retirement. However, he may be recalled to active duty at the military's discretion until after he has completed another 10 years of inactive reserve duty to complete the full 30-year term. For many, the 10-year mark is an important point, when they feel the need to decide whether to stay on active duty for the entire 20 years or leave the service. Such was the case with Chief Andrews. At his 10-year mark, he had attained the rank of first-class petty officer — one rank below the level of Chief. Although he was still vacillating between striving to achieve the rank of Chief or trying again for an officer commissioning program, because he viewed himself as being "right on the threshold" of the rank of Chief, he decided to remain enlisted and strive to become a Chief. He added that his remembrance of the Chiefs who had mentored him affected his decision to work toward becoming a Chief.

While he seemed to value the mentors who helped him, he stated that, as he came through the ranks, he had not heard of the Navy's formal mentorship program. However, as he looks back over his career, he can see and value the role informal mentors played in advancing his career:

> I never used the word "mentor" until I came to my current command. This was the first command where we had a mentor program in writing. So it was folks that I naturally gravitated to. Over time I looked back and said, "Okay that person was my mentor; Senior Chief so and so was a mentor to me." Where I'm currently stationed is really where they had a mentor program and used that word. I had never used that word before now.... I tell folks one of the most influential mentors that I had was not someone that was on my job. I think it's important to have someone removed from your day to day grind that can give you a point of view on life, building relationships (professional & personal), and personal development. I owe my own successes in the Navy to those folks that helped me. Who took the time to say "this kid has some potential; let me see what I can do to keep him from going down the wrong path."

Chief Andrews also expressed the belief that race did not affect the quality of his mentorship. When asked to describe how he perceived the quality of mentorship White male sailors received when compared to that provided to African American male sailors, he stated "I don't think race had much to do with it. I had a couple of mentors that were White and very influential. One Master Chief I worked for didn't see color. I think very highly of him."

He went on to describe steps in his career that he believed were more difficult than others. When asked about this, he stated that, while he was promoted relatively quickly, any difficulties that he had were within himself. When asked if there were any obstacles external to himself, he responded,

> I worked with the kind of people that I didn't necessarily agree with or that were Chiefs or first class. [I said] "If that's how they are, then I don't want to be a Chief." I guess that was part of the reason why I hadn't decided if I was going to be an officer either because I saw so many examples of people wearing uniforms and I'm like, "I don't necessarily want to be that way."

He added that there were times when he thought of quitting. He gave an example of a time when, earlier in his career, he was thinking of not making the Navy a career because of some of the people he worked with. He stated that he did not think that the Navy or the people he worked with were helping him to make decisions regarding his career. It was his financial situation that eventually led to his final decision to stay. When asked if there were any other factors that played a role in helping him make this final decision to stay, he added,

> I met a Master Chief who took me under his wing a long time ago. He told me basically the uniform doesn't define who you are. You'll define the uniform. Just because you are wearing a certain uniform doesn't mean you have to be a certain way. You use your position to enhance who you are and that in turn will make you a better Chief, officer, or sailor.

Although he eventually met a Master Chief who helped him, he stated that negative feelings lingered after he made Chief:

> Oh yeah. I wanted to track those folks down and show up to say "Ha now. All that negativity you spewed at me, look at me now." After some thought, I thought that's not who I am. I've never been that type of person. What good would come of it?

Instead, he found a more positive way to dispose of those negative feelings. Discussing how he turned those experiences into a positive by viewing them as a learning experience, he stated,

> Yes. Like I said, I had to look at it as a learning experience. You have people in your life that are there to help you out, motivate you, to pick you up when you are down. I had to come to a realization that everyone I came across is a teacher, whether they want to be or don't want to be. So if I look at it like that then I say, "Well, there are all the negative things I didn't like about this person. Let me not incorporate those into my makeup. Maybe that will make me a better person for it." In hindsight 20/20 after a couple years reflection, I can't say I was thinking like that when going through those experiences. Looking back at it, I've come to that conclusion. I don't hold the same animosity that I had towards them as I did when I was going through with them.

Another factor that was examined in this interview was the extent to which this participant was able to fit in and be accepted as equal to his White peers. He stated that although he believes he fits in, he never really cared about that very much. He added that he does have friends who are White. Further, he discussed how he believes he has altered his communication patterns in order to fit into the predominantly White organization:

> I guess the biggest thing I can think of when asked that question is the manner of speak[ing]. Sometimes you talk in a relaxed/slang type tone. Where

you're dealing with folks that may not necessarily know what you are talking about. So that's an obstacle. I'm more at home with a couple of Black officers where I can speak the way I would speak to my sailors. I mean in a casual format where they understand what I'm talking about. If I were to speak that same way towards a White officer, Chief, Master Chief or whatever, [he] would not take to what I was saying. Instead of hearing the message, they would hear the sender. That can cause and has caused some conflict and confusion. That's the biggest thing I can think of.

In addition to altering his communications to fit in with some Whites, he also stated that he is careful about being sensitive to the types of music that is played in the workplace. He expressed concern for being sensitive to the diverse cultures present:

I'm consistent on that and as far as music or anything like that is concerned. I like rap music and there is a lot of rap songs that deal with cursing. I've never been the type to blast that stuff during the day.... Because we're in a diverse culture, you gotta be careful not to play something that some will take as offensive. I tell my folks the same thing. Just because they like it, you gotta be aware of others' sensitivity. It's more along the lines of how I would communicate with someone.

When the conversation turned to how his competence is viewed, he expressed no doubt about being equally competent to his peers. However, he did express some doubt about whether his supervisors and others accept him as being equally competent. When asked about this, he stated,

I have no doubt that I'm just as competent as the person standing next to me. They might not think so. I don't think I'm incompetent or can't measure up to someone because they happen to be a White male or anything like that.

Regarding whether he believed others, such as supervisors, accepted him to be equally competent, he added,

Probably not; because I'm a young Black male. I sometimes believe there are those that are particularly in a leadership or management position that second guess or don't be taking me seriously. I think it's a combination of my race and age.

I asked Chief Andrews for his views on how race may have affected his promotions as he progressed up the ranks toward Chief. He seemed to believe that race was not a factor in his own promotion but did not rule it out as a possible factor in the careers of others:

For me race wasn't an issue because the advancement process is driven solely on an advancement exam. Well not solely but it's a portion. Some of the contributing factors towards your advancement are your advancement exam, evaluation, awards. Maybe those things may cause someone to be adversely affected when it comes times for advancement. Personally I've never had that issue because I advanced pretty quickly. I can't honestly use race as a determining factor. I've heard minorities tend to advance quicker in the military ... particularly get selected for different programs. I haven't seen concrete evidence to substantiate those claims.

Although he stated that he didn't believe that race was much of a factor in his promotion, he did allude to the possibility that bias could impact the Navy's evaluation process. When asked if race may have advantaged or disadvantaged him in the evaluation process with respect to White sailors, he stated,

It's kind of hard to say since the evaluation process is still subjective. It's one person's opinion on how you are as a performer. Obviously none of my supervisors said, "Well because you're Black this is what I think of you." It would set them up for trouble. I can't think of any case where my race had any negative factors.

While Chief Andrews stated that he could not think of cases where race negatively affected his career, he did contemplate how it could be a positive factor for African American men:

The military is still predominantly a White male organization. So maybe to some degree there is the element of surprise. "Wow I didn't know this guy was going to perform at a level, so let's reward him." That's purely an opinion.

Moreover, he provided a concrete example of two sailors—one Black and one White—who worked for him. In this example he believed the Black sailor, who was equally deserving, was denied due recognition—not necessarily based on race—but based on other non-merit factors. In his own words,

I've got a White female and a Black male sailor. Both of them work very hard and both of them are good sailors. However, the young Black male sailor has the perception that he's a thug. Part of it is his fault. When I say his fault [it's] because I've sat down and talked to him. I said "you've got to understand there is a time and place for everything." When you hang out with friends, you can speak that way. You can't carry that over when you're walking up and down the hallways or p-ways on the ship. Those same people see this female White sailor who every time they see her she's speaking properly. She's addressing people. He's walking around singing rap songs, this that and the third. It's your own way of success. When I submitted these two names for quarterly awards, one—the White female sailor—no problem, absolutely she's great. The Black male sailor, they looked at me like, "You must be kidding, this guy is a thug, this guy is lazy, this guy is.... There is no way I would have this guy as representing a command." Yes he warranted recognition but the perception by those that made the ultimate decision is what kept him from being awarded. Part of it is his fault. I would say to some degree you have to play the game a little bit. You gotta play by their rules to get what you need to attain.

He added,

> I feel that both sailors merit the recognition. However because one is more acceptable.... He knows his job, deals well with senior officers, commanding officers. The people in the know don't see that. I see that. So because merit is ... he's not being fully recognized for his work ethic. I can tell it's frustrating because he thinks that I'm not doing what I gotta do to help him get there. [He thinks] I'm not supporting him or fighting for him. It's very hard to overcome a perception one has of you despite your best efforts.

Chief Andrews also expressed an understanding — almost sympathy — for why the African American male sailors do not change the way they present themselves to their supervisors:

> They don't want to be accused of selling out. I don't blame [them] for not wanting to sell out who they are. There's a compromise you have to make within yourself. At the same time, you're going to ask [them to be] somebody that's totally different from what they are. I don't want to change who I am just because my Chief thought I was a thug or my Chief thought just because I was a Black man that I didn't amount to nothing. I [don't] want to change who I am as a person, but strike a balance of keeping my individuality but prove I'm more than what you think I am.

When I asked Chief Andrews to provide any additional stories or examples that would help me understand his experiences in the Navy, he provided the following story of one of his experiences:

> I had this one Chief on my last ship, White guy. He told me I would never make Chief. I'm just a thug. That's something that's not even in my make up. I used that as fuel to say, "Hey you can't judge someone based on appearance," and second I use that anger towards him to buckle down and prove him wrong. That's one of my biggest influences to making Chief. Even though I don't think that was his desire. He wanted to see me fail and in turn I wanted to prove him wrong. I wanted to make sure that I wasn't that kind of person, to automatically assume I know a certain person based on their outward appearance. I had that same type of feeling towards the young Black male sailor that I was talking about earlier until I got to know him. I never said anything to him like you're just a thug, you'll never be this or you'll never be that. I had my own impressions of him until I got to know him. I guess I have an extra interest in making sure this young man does not encounter the same situations, same people that I have. I don't want him to compromise who he is as a person. At the same time I don't want him to get in his own way when it comes time to be considered for evaluations, citations, awards, advancements, the whole nine.

Discussing what he perceives as the plight of the young African American male sailor, this participant added,

> You got kids that are ... like I said nobody joins the military to get kicked out or go UA or do anything that's going ... I don't know of any sailor that I've ever talked to when they first come in the military that have goals of getting kicked out of the military. So you've got good kids being kicked out. You got kids that got the potential but aren't being considered or [being] taken [and] considered [as if] they got something to bring to the table. If you tell me I'm a dirt bag enough times I'm either going to make you right or use that as fuel into the opposite. If you don't have people in your corner to guide you through those steps then you're just going to say, "Well shit, he's calling me a dirt bag all these times. I guess I am a dirt bag; I guess I'm a thug. So since I'm a thug let me go smoke some weed; let me go knock over a liquor store. Let me go [do] this or let me go do that." I know I'm going extreme in [this] example but I see it, especially on a ship my size. You see that a lot more commonly than you do in a smaller command or smaller division.

Finally, Chief Andrews commented on his views of how White sailors experience the Navy:

> I don't think that they feel they have to be Black for me to understand them. I really can't speak from their point of view because I've never been a White sailor going through the ranks. I can only speak from another Black sailor's point of view. I don't know what type of obstacles or encounters they have to go through. I don't know if they're perceived as being smarter or better at being a sailor. I've seen dirt bags come in all shapes and colors. I've seen good sailors come in all shapes and colors too. I don't know what types of obstacles they have to encounter. I wouldn't think there would be that many at all since society itself is predominantly White male. So if you're a White male going into something then you got a leg up. That's my opinion. You can slack off a little bit whereas a young Black or Hispanic sailor has to bust their butt a little harder to eliminate any type of perceptions that are there already. My opinion.

Chief Butler

Chief Butler joined the Navy in 1989. Growing up the oldest of six children in a single-parent household, he learned responsibility at a very young age. He stated that, to help his mother, he would help get his younger brothers and sisters ready for school, cook them food, and do other things to help around the house. Unlike many of the participants in this study, he stated that he had known that he would enlist in the Navy since he was 8 years old. He was inspired by the structure he had observed when attending his uncle's Navy basic training graduation in 1978, 11 years before he was old enough to enlist. Reflecting on observing his uncle during the graduation ceremony, he noted, "I was overcome by the amount of structure and discipline in that whole ceremony and how good he looked and how happy he looked to be doing something different than being in the neighborhood we were in.... It was my uncle Tony who was the reason I joined the Navy."

Although he knew he would join, he stated that he was not certain that he would make the Navy a career. However, he did know that he was happy to leave the circumstances that he was in as he was growing up. Being a Chief was not one of his career aspirations during his early years in the Navy. Instead, after being assigned to Naval Air Station Lemoore and working around A-7 aircraft, he had decided that he wanted to be a Navy pilot. However, as time progressed and he formed opinions about Navy officers, he changed his mind. In his own words,

> And then, you know, as I grew older and had more experience I realized that I didn't want to have anything to do with the officer ranks. And I began setting my sights on just going as far as an enlisted man as I could because I like being an enlisted man. I did not like the arrogance that I saw in a lot of the pilots and it was easier for me to be around people that I thought I could relate to better. As far as being a career, you know, I ... in my opinion I'd rather not sacrifice happiness for money.

At that point he set out to get as far as he could as an enlisted man and this meant striving to attain the rank of Chief, Senior Chief, or Master Chief.

He acknowledges difficulties as he worked toward achieving the highest enlisted rank that he could. Some of these difficulties, he stated, he created for himself, while others were external to him. Depicting this, he offered the following illustration:

> You know I'm an inner-city guy from Chicago and you know the streets ... will probably always be in me, to tell the truth about it. And a lot of times when I get to my first place or first command I would have to turn that type of thing off so people can give me a fair shake. Ah I remember when I got to A-school I intentionally was missing out on duty section musters and all that kinda stuff 'cause remember I'm this tough Chicago kid. So I would go to up to some other junior enlisted guy who was the section leader for that weekend and say, "Hey look, dude, I ain't standing no watches." And it would pretty much go down like that till one of my A-school instructors caught wind of that.

He then discussed how an intervention by a more senior African American sailor affected him:

And I'll never forget his name. It's AO1 Bragg. This cat come to me. I'm sittin' in my room in the barracks there and he goes ... "Hey, where you been all weekend?" And I told him and he commenced to giving me a good lecture and he told me straight up. He said, "You know, there's a lot of stereotypes out there and right now you're supporting a bunch of 'em. And it's up to you whether you want to, you know, make your career like that or not. But believe you me, people are going to judge you as soon as they see you and then you're going to have to work after that to either prove 'em right or prove 'em wrong." That was some good advice that I kept with me. I still keep it with me. As far as work goes, actually it's been partly me and partly the attitude for the rate I'm in. I mean, to be an AO [Aviation Ordnanceman] you have to be a member of a team. As a young kid I've always played sports, football, basketball, so the team concept is really something that I've embraced all my life. And I don't know, after walking in the door and showing people that I can lead teams and I possess the ability to absorb knowledge and remember it and apply it to whatever situation, whether it was regular day-to-day ops or wartime ops, I became one of those reliable dependable people that they could just not do without. And to me that was the key to me advancing, become that person that people would say, "I don't care what you do but we got to have ... [him] with me."

As he continued discussing what he perceived as obstacles he had to face in advancing through the Navy ranks, he discussed an incident with one of his supervisors and how that incident affected him:

My very first duty station was kinda like that, you know. And I remember walking in the door and my first class there was telling me, and I'm sure this was his speech to everybody, all new check-in's. I remember him telling me the type of things he would and would not tolerate ... all of those laziness and being to work on time and all that kinda thing and I remember ... taking offense to that because I'm like, "Wait, this guy don't know me from Adam" ... and after that moment I made up in my mind that I'm gonna be the best worker here. I'm gonna be the best looking in my uniform, I'm gonna know the most, and I'm gonna be able to apply it better than anybody at this joint. I made that happen.

As we continued our conversations, he discussed how things changed, but remained the same, as he progressed up the ranks to senior petty officer and eventually to Chief:

As you go higher, of course things change. You know, when they ... when they start seeing chevrons on your sleeves then there are expectations that they have for you as far as work performance. On the other side of that, then there is the liberty side of that as well. And I do know personally that at work, I was a great guy and everybody wanted me around, but on liberty some of those same people that I sweated with quite a bit getting work done, they didn't want to hang out with me on liberty. And as I became a Chief, that became really evident to me in a couple [of] different commands I was in. You know, people, they would always love me at the DRBs [disciplinary review boards] and stuff because you know as a former RDC [recruit division commander], I had quite a bit of experience at getting in somebody's butt. But, when it came liberty time, we lived in the same berthing, in the same area in the berthing, and I would notice 'em all getting ready to go somewhere and all this kinda stuff but I can remember maybe once in two deployments that they said hey, you want to come roll with us. And that didn't bother me. It just made me realize that I was cool to hang with at work but off work I wasn't their type of guy and I was fine with that. I still am fine with that.

He went on to discuss why he believed the other sailors excluded him from their social events:

Well, it could be a combination of things. I think it ... that we could possibly have some things in common. You know, ah ... sometimes sailors do what sailors do you know and when we go out on liberty ... I would say the majority, at least 51% of folks, like to go somewhere and have a good meal and you know have a few drinks and whatever the case may be and play it from ear or maybe go on a tour or whatever the case may be. That being said, I don't know if they didn't think I like to do those kinda things or what but I do know that I had to find my own group of people to go and hang out with.

I asked him if making Chief had any significant impact on how often he was invited out with his colleagues. He responded,

Oh no. What's different, my first sea tour after I put on khakis was in prowler squadrons. And of course there aren't many AOCs. There's only one AO Chief so you're kinda out there on your own anyhow. But these other Chiefs would just ... they would kinda treat me that way because, partly because I think in my mind is that prowlers are used to doing things, ordnance-wise, different than other communities that do things. They don't, take as much care handling explosives as they should. Me being new to that community at the time, I didn't tolerate it. I did what was ... what was in the book and, and I wouldn't bend. And sometimes that hindered their ability to get the airplane airborne as fast as [they] would like. In my mind that wasn't my problem. In my mind I was doing what, exactly what the Navy was paying me to do. And so I had no problem with that. And I think that had a little bit do with ... why ... I didn't get as many invites to go hang out with 'em socially.

He continued on this topic:

I would probably say ... I don't know. It could have been the way I looked, the way I dressed. Because you know I still dress like, like I would normally dress when I'm back home. I wear jeans, I wear t-shirts. I mean they wear jeans and t-shirts but different styles. Different styles, you know, there's ... there's ... everybody's got their own styles, whatever that may be, and I think my style was not a fit with their style. You know they were going to hang out at a bar and listen to some country music whereas I can do some country music for a little bit but I don't intend to do that my whole ... all the time that I have liberty.

At this point, I asked Chief Butler if, in describing these experiences and his beliefs in why they occurred they way the did, he was dancing around the issue of race. He responded,

I probably am. But I think there are some racial ... there were some racial things involved with it as well. Since I've been a Chief, everywhere I've been, I've been the only Black khaki there. Everywhere I've been. And that ... it sometimes, you know, it may be me ... I don't know. Or it may be the rest of my peer group. But I have expectations as well. You know, I, when I walk in the door somewhere I give the benefit of the doubt to everybody there. You know I think that people are people regardless of who they are, where they come from, religious background or any of that.... Sometimes I wonder if people think that, that I have got some sort of different agenda. You know, because I don't. I think I'm the average American who happens to who happens to have ... people have a different opinion after they see me or hear my name or something like that. You know how the Chief community is. People know well before you do who you are if you're coming to their command. They've already talked to somebody who knows you or knows of you or something like that. And if they don't recognize the name they'll, they'll find out. You know, they'll find out what kind of guy you are and what kind of work you do. And my name is pretty.... it's kinda easy to realize that I'm probably not Caucasian if you see my name ... come up on orders.

After discussing what he perceived as barriers and his subjective views of why he was treated the way he was, I asked him if he ever thought of quitting. He responded,

Usually on deployment. Those were pretty much the only times. And it would be pretty much during really, really hard days ... you know, missing my kids and missing my family or something like that but that's all it was. It was just being homesick in the back of my mind, you know. You know, you being a former Chief, there's pretty much only one place you can really go and relax when you're out there, and that's in your rack. You know, those feelings I would get about maybe I want to find another career or something where I can be home or something like that. Those were really the only times it would come to me, was those nights when I was finally resting in my rack or something like that. But as a whole, I've never really thought about quitting. As a whole, I've enjoyed my job. I've really enjoyed being an ordnanceman. I enjoy the Navy, you know, for the most part. I think there are some things, that have happened in recent years I have discomfort with, or I don't probably agree with, but as a whole I like the job.

Based on his comments, he seemed to believe that his thoughts of quitting were not caused by how he was treated in the Navy. When asked if his treatment by his peers ever caused him to think of quitting, he responded,

> Oh no, not ever, because they don't feed my family. You know that ... I don't ... I don't put much, if any concern in that area at all. You know at the end of the day, they don't pay my paycheck. So I don't ... I'm not concerned with them not even a little bit.

Our conversation moved on to his feelings about making Chief. He stated that he was very happy, but at the same time, he thought he should have been promoted to Chief earlier than he actually was. I asked him to elaborate on that point and he explained,

> Well, the reason that I thought it should have happened to me a couple years before that is because my record has been outstanding since day one you know I can prove it with my service record. My evals have always been excellent ... not excellent, they have always been outstanding. I've always performed well everywhere I've gone and ... it took me 3 times to do it [make Chief]. But you see, it's not the Navy's fault that it should have happened to me a couple years before this. Actually, it's my fault because no one had ever taught me how to verify my service record against my microfiche. There were some significant errors in my stuff and I remember when I put it on, I was at RTC Great Lakes. I was pushing boots [serving as a recruit division commander] at the time and the Chief that was pushing the division across the passageway from me, he was the only guy who came over and said, "...what's going on with you, kid. Let me take a look at your record." So he straightened me out and after that, things have moved pretty nicely.

I asked him if any negative feelings lingered once he was finally selected for Chief. Initially, he said he did not have any negative feelings, but then after rethinking his response, he added,

> Nah, I take that back. I did have one. The only one I had was I wish all of those people that said I was a good guy, and all that, had told me how to verify my service record against what was on my microfiche. But other than that I didn't have any negative feelings. No [I didn't have any other negative feelings], because the couple people I really had issue with, I made Chief before they did anyway. To me it was not that I had any ill will or bad feelings toward them. I just kinda thought to myself that "we see ... now we see what ... you know cream rises to the top and I made it before you." So it was kinda a little personal ... you know me kinda poking at 'em a little bit.

Chief Butler expressed pride in his accomplishments as a Chief. He seemed particularly proud of his impact on young enlisted sailors during his time as a recruit division commander. He believes that his influence on them helped many of them to be successful in their own careers. In his own words,

So my feelings about what I've done as a Chief in that aspect I'm really proud of. I really do think that I transitioned some civilians into sailors who are gonna be productive and it's evident by ... you know, seeing.... I've ran into quite a few of 'em. Some of 'em are officers now ... some of 'em are Chiefs now like I am ... you know those that are nuclear propulsion types. But think I've done a really good job of telling those guys what they can expect, prepared them for the Navy life and how they need to work diligently. They need to climb a success ladder, if that's what they want to do. So sailorization in that way, that's just one part of it. You know in different commands, I've done all kinds of things as far as helping people retake ASVABs and be accepted into programs, making sure people earn their wings and holding people's feet to the fire so they work hard and study hard so they can advance.

In addition to the impact he believes he has had on young sailors' careers, Chief Butler also discussed his views on his accomplishments as a technician and as a role model for other African American sailors:

I've done quite a bit since I've been, you know, up here at Whidbey Island. There wasn't even an ordnance training program on this base until I got here. I started that ... or I brought it back to life, let me say that. I didn't start it; I brought it back to life. So I think I've done quite a bit professionally. Personally, with a lot of people, because not only do I think I have a responsibility as a Navy Chief, I have a responsibility as a Black man as well. Going back to that whole AO1 Bragg issue I was talking about. You see, that guy didn't have to come to my room and tell me to stop screwing up. That was something he did so he can make sure at least I had a fighting chance. And when I do see these, you know, a lot of our younger brothers and sisters, you know racially speaking, and they're screwing up, I try to get 'em back on the right path and sometimes I'm successful and sometimes I'm not. But even Jesus Christ couldn't save everybody so I'm not concerned about that. The ones that I did save and get 'em on the right path, I'm very proud of that.

He clearly believes he has made a significant impact on the Navy and on the lives of young sailors. This was expressed, not only in his words, but also in the passion with which he spoke. However, when asked if he felt his superiors properly rewarded him for his accomplishments, he responded,

Do I think it's at the level it should be? No. But I have [been rewarded] you know. Since I've become a Chief I've had three Navy Achievements. I think I've ... some of the things I think I've done I should have been accommodated for you know, a Navy Comm, you know. As well as being the ordnance Chief in the command, I was the first guy to accept the brand new mod of airplane. Some of the other people that were in that same command, they were showing me the coin that the skipper gave them. You know, to say that they developed the first ICAP III aircraft and accepted the first ICAP III aircraft and I'm, like wow, I was the sole maintenance controller, with no others, and the skipper didn't give me one of those coins. He didn't even give me an end of tour award. When it was time to go, he just let me go. And I've been awarded but my rewards don't come really in medals and paper because not everybody's going to pat you on the back. My rewards come in seeing those people I was mentioning earlier be successful to get past whatever stereotype might be out there because in my experience in the Navy, there's one thing that speaks for you louder than anything else, that's work performance. If you can prove to people that you're the top notch as far as work goes, they tend to stop forgetting what you look like because they know what you do.

Although this participant indicated that he does not believe he has received recognition commensurate with what he has accomplished, he does not attribute this to anything associated with race. Instead, he suggests that conflict with commanding officers and executive officers has caused him to receive less recognition than he believes he has earned. When asked if he has pondered the issue, he replied:

Oh yea, I've given it a lot of thought. Some of the things I thought about was I think I did have personal differences between my COs and XOs. There were a lot of things that I didn't allow them to do ... or I would tell them because it's their squadron you know. The CO can do whatever he wants to do in his squadron pretty much but I would damn sure make sure I present him his options, you know. Sometimes he didn't like how I had to say it but I thought it was my job to tell him because if I don't tell him, nobody will and if he got caught screwing up then he could be in trouble or she could be in trouble. I think as a Chief, that's my job. Sometimes somebody does need to tell 'em the things that they don't want to hear or don't like to hear. But that was me. I would tell 'em what, what's going on.

In spite of believing he did not receive rewards that were commensurate with his contributions to the Navy, Chief Butler believes he has accomplished all the professional goals he has set for himself. He does believe, however, that there are personal goals that remain unfulfilled and that he is working toward fulfilling those:

No, all the accomplishments that I wish I had done are all personal. Navy wise I don't think I'm leaving anything out there at all. I try to give it all I've got every day. The only accomplishments that I wish I could have achieved or that I'm still working toward achieving are all personal, whether that be my own personal education or, you know, having more time to be a better father to my children whatever the case may be. But none of 'em are out there as far as professional.

Consistent with this assertion that he has accomplished all his professional goals, Chief Butler was adamant that, if given the opportunity to start his career over again, he would not change anything. Further, he emphasized the need to be authentic and suggested that doing things differently would equate to not being authentic. Regarding doing things differently, he stated,

> I wouldn't, because it wouldn't be me. I look at it again, the reason I don't ... I would never want to be an officer. I don't think that I need to compromise who I am to get a job done. It irks me to no end to have to fit in and I don't think I should have to make any special efforts to fit in and I won't do it ... don't get me wrong, I'm not saying I may go out of my way to stand out, because I don't. But I'm not gonna play golf because I don't play golf. I'm not gonna do the things that are not of interest to me just to be a part of a group. That's just how I am.

The focus of our conversation then shifted to the topic of mentorship. Earlier in the interview he had alluded to informal mentorship that he had provided to other young sailors and which he had received from others. He seemed to believe that mentorship is important to succeeding in the Navy. Here, again, he stressed this point:

> I think it is. I think mentorship is definitely something that is required because so many people — especially young people — I hate for them to lose their way. And even more pertinent, so many young people don't even have a way yet. They are just here because ... for different reasons. Mainly a lot of it is because they have nothing else to do so that's why they are around. So mentorship is a very simple tool for helping people advance and get to the places they need to be. Ah, personally, I didn't require a lot of mentorship. I still don't require a lot of mentorship. I think ... I have two ... well I have a couple driving factors. Well one is all based around family. Which is, you know, the family that I grew up with — my mother, my uncle and my grandmother and myself— and I think my worst fear is being considered a failure to those people. And that's what drives ... that's [what] I think that is the main thing that drives me to wanna do my best.... I never wanna be ... I don't wanna be a failure.

He then reflected on his own career and the mentors he has had. The subject of mentorship was clearly personal to Chief Butler and this point came through in his discussion of his own mentors and why he considered them mentors:

> You know I'm trying to think about that right now and I'm just running through supervisors that I've had before. And I've had.... I've probably had a couple but that was a long time ago. That was back when I was an airman. And at the time I had a couple guys that were second classes that I looked up to because they seemed to, you know, they seemed to have their lives together ... the Senior Chief I had. And their mentorship it wasn't professional. I think the reason I looked up to 'em so is because it appeared that their life was in order and from the disorder that I came from before I was in the Navy, I craved that. I wanted to have stability. I wanted to have ... a life that was ...

that somebody would remember when I'm gone. That's why I looked up to those guys.

Although he was clear about the importance he places on mentorship, he seemed significantly less enthusiastic about the Navy's formal mentorship program. When asked about this formal program and whether he has a formally assigned mentor, he replied, "We had ... that's, that's policy now. That's everywhere. Yea, I have one ... I have someone's name on a piece of paper." I then asked him to rate the quality of the mentorship provided by his formally assigned mentor. He responded,

> You know I can't answer that because I haven't given that person an opportunity to be a mentor ... basically because I'm arrogant enough to think that I don't need one. But, I'm sure he'd be a great mentor. I mean he's a couple pay grades higher than I am and everybody knows that many people have tried to become a Master Chief but not everybody gets there. So you know I'm sure he's got things that he can teach me or tell me but I just—I probably haven't given him the opportunity to push me in the direction I need to go.

He offered a totally different view of his experiences with informal mentors. When asked to elaborate on his experiences with informal mentors, he offered the following:

> Oh yes, definitely. A couple of those. There's a ... the ordnance handling officer on the USS *Kitty Hawk*. You know at one point that guy used to be my LPO and now he's a commander. And not just that he's advanced in that way but I really respect him as a man. He's a good guy. And he's got the ordnance community's best interest at heart with whatever he does. You know, whether you're gonna like his decision or not, you know what it's based on. And then that, I respect him greatly. So he's an indirect mentor of mine. And my other one of course is my uncle, who's a retired Chief but he's been a mentor of mine since I was, since I was a baby. As far as I'm concerned, for a father figure, he's pretty much all I've ever had, so he will always be a mentor. You know again, he's the whole reason I joined the Navy in the first place so he, he's still a mentor of mine.

After discussing the role formal and informal mentors had in his own career development, I asked him whether he had been a mentor in the lives of other sailors. In discussing this issue, he shared with me the types of issues his protégés would bring to him and the general advice he provided:

> Oh yea. Lots of people ... but I get lots, you know, my, my guys come and see me nearly, nearly every day you know, to talk about issues they have at work and why they feel like they might not be getting qualifications that they're qualified for and all those types of things and you know. I tell 'em that sometimes it's a process, you know, some of the things I was saying before.

Don't let people hinder you from being where you wanna be. Sometimes they'll put obstacles and roadblocks in front of you but have the fortitude to, to wait it out. Wait 'em out. Keep doing what you need to do and eventually they'll, they'll see that you're somebody worthy to give the qualification to.

Discussing whether he believes the mentorship he provided other sailors made a difference, he was clear in asserting his belief that it did. Further, he suggested that he believed that his race enhanced the quality of the mentorship he provided to young African American sailors:

> I do. Wholeheartedly. Not only because, you know, sometimes I get to see 'em be successful but I think it's important because some of those people have no one else to turn to ... somebody Black in somewhat of a power position. Some of the things they come and talk to me about, they're personal things. Some of the things they come and talk to me about are largely professional things. But they, off site they think they can relate to me in that way. And it's true, they can. I can relate to where they're coming from. And it's good to, to me it's good to have someone to talk to, to express your concerns. If I can be there just, just as a person listening. If I don't open my mouth to give 'em any advice on what they should do, just being a person that can hear what they're saying and understand where they're coming from, that's already part of the battle. I think that serves a role as well.

I queried him further on the issue of race, asking him what role, if any, he believes race has had in his promotion. His response was somewhat surprising:

> I think it has played some role in my advancement. I think as far as making Chief it has. I can't say this for certain because I don't know as much about ah equal opportunity programs as I probably should, but I'm almost certain that there is a quota of what type of people that they're suppose to select. They're supposed to select so many Pacific Islanders; they're supposed to select so many African Americans and females and you know Hispanics and so forth and so on. So do I think that it has had some impact? Of course I do. I think my record already spoke for itself but for me to be Black and to be and to have all the checks in the block that they were looking for, it was perfect.

While he believed race had a positive impact on his promotion to Chief, he stated that race was not a factor — either positive or negative — in lower pay grades. He explained it this way:

> No. Personally I don't. And the reason is because all the advancements before Chief is a test. You know and what do they figure into that ... how well I performed on that test and my performance factor on my evaluation. And I always knew that my.... I'm in control of my evaluations. People can ... they can try to deny me but everybody in that command will know that I deserved what I got because I, I try to be that good ... without stabbing people in the

back. I think you know as far as the test and the performance factor, I think race had nothing to do with that.

He tended to view the promotion process as relatively egalitarian in the lower pay grades and actually tilted toward minorities in the higher enlisted grades. However, when our conversation shifted to his views about whether he fits in with his White peers, he painted a much different picture of the impact of race:

> That's a good question. Ah, wow, that one's got me quiet. In some ways, in some ways I don't. You know, and here's why. When people describe me — and I'm only saying this because I've heard it — they can describe other people in the Chief's mess and they'll say, "Chief this guy, Chief this guy" and somebody will say "Chief who?" and they'll be like "You know, this guy." But when they describe me, it's always "You know him, that Black Chief." And then they're like, "Oh yea, I know who you're talking about." You know what I mean? So I know in that way I don't feel like I fit in. And in other ways I ... well as far as why I feel like I don't fit in or things are a little bit more difficult for me within the peer group, let's take in a board like we're doing input to a sailor of the quarter, sailor of the year, any award, something like that. And this is where I think that there's a problem. When I have to speak for somebody, I have to be dramatic; it has to have full impact for anybody to, to, to give any credit or validation to what I'm saying. I can't simply come into a room and say, "This guy's doing well because he did this, therefore I nominate him." If I did that, a lot of the people I represent would get jack. And I've seen it done. I've really seen it done. So, when it's time for those things I really have to do homework and I have to practice what I'm gonna say to the rest of my brothers in the Chiefs' mess for impact. I have to be dramatic about it for them to get their fair shake. And I've seen that ... that's just been my experience on way more than one occasion.

In further amplifying his response, he added,

> My personal thought is I think they discredit a lot of things ... I'm saying because for some reason they may think that I'm not as smart as they are ... that my ability to evaluate somebody's performance is not as good as their ability to evaluate somebody's performance. That's what I think. I don't know. And that usually happens ... well it happens with everybody I put up, but if I'm putting up somebody Black or somebody Latino or something like that, I think ... they.... in my opinion the first think that comes to my mind is, "He just wants to get an award for another minority ... he just wants another minority to be the sailor of the quarter." That's what I think. Because you can.... I can see the looks in their eyes when I mention the person's name. It's like they want to dismiss the entire thing as soon as I say their name.

To further show how other Chiefs' perception of him affects the sailors who work for him, he provided a scenario that he believes clearly illustrates the point. He explained,

I was the Division Chief for a guy and I wanted to make this guy sailor of the quarter and I got fought tooth and nail about how screwed up this guy was. I checked out of the command and the same guy that they wouldn't make sailor of the quarter is now sailor of the year ... after somebody else is their Division Chief and he hadn't done anything different, the same qualifications, the whole bit, but the same guy who was not good enough for the sailor of the quarter is the sailor of the year of the command. That blew me away.

Earlier, in this interview, Chief Butler expressed his view that race was not a factor in promotions in the lower pay grades and that the promotion process was based on merit. However, when asked if the careers of his subordinate sailors were impacted by how his peers viewed him, he responded,

I, I ... it likely has some effect on their ability to promote, because with those things, of course they can promote without being a sailor of the quarter or sailor of the year. But, does it help? Of course it helps. And I want to give my ... the people that are, you know, directly under me every opportunity that they deserve. So does that bother me? That bothers me greatly because like I told you before, I don't necessarily care what people think about me. That doesn't bother me at all. But it bothers me that because of what they think about me it has an effect on people under me. That tears, that burns me. That chaps my ass. Yea, it does. That can have an effect on it.

Our conversation then turned to Chief Butler's view of the degree to which the Navy has succeeded in integrating people of different races and the degree to which the Navy has created a meritocracy. Discussing his own views of how well the Navy has done in integrating people from different racial backgrounds, he stated,

My views on that is, I wouldn't call it a success story, but I would say it's the most forward thinking of a lot of our society. You've gotta keep in mind the military is nothing but a mix of society that's already out there in the world. So people already come in with their preconceived notions, whatever they may be. Because we are, one, directed to by instruction to give people those opportunities it happens. And, secondly, there's a different respect level people have for one another once you are deployed. When you go out on a deployment and people see you got heart and you'll do whatever or what needs to be done to make a mission happen, you earn a different sort of respect that our civilian counterparts ... they're not privileged enough to see that. You know the type of pressure that that can put you under, people know what you're made of and once they find out what you're made of then there's a different respect level. So in that way, the military is quite a bit [more] advanced than, you know, the civilian counterparts out there.

Regarding the military's claim of meritocracy, he added,

> I wouldn't say it's accurate, 100% accurate that your abilities are the only things that speak for you. Because I know a lot of morons that have made rate, so I wouldn't say it's all ability. A lot of it has to do with who you know too. Quite a bit, I would say. But your, for the most part, ability is a ... the major determinant factor if you're going to advance or not. Again, my views are the military has had a large success in that manner because people are put into high pressure positions. You know those people, the marines and army dogs that are over there on the ground you know dodging bullets together. That type of thing has the ability to bring people together no matter what they look like. If they had five arms and they were green and they were on the same team and were fighting for their lives together, then of course there's gonna ... that's gonna form a camaraderie that's, that's gonna be hard to break no matter what people look like. So the military's claim, if they're saying that policy is what's done that, I disagree. You know you can ... admirals and senators and everybody can put on paper whatever they want but people are gonna still think whatever they wanna think. They're free to do so but when you are in those high stress situations that is what brings people together and makes people realize I'm not so different from you.

Chief Carter

Chief Carter stated that he joined the Navy "mainly to get away and see the world." His initial intentions were not to make the Navy a career. He expected to serve the required 3 years of active duty and perhaps promote to third-class petty officer [E-4]. He was aware of the many benefits offered by the military and stated that he wanted to capitalize on those and then leave the service after his first enlistment. However, he did stay beyond his first enlistment and served two terms. It was after his second enlistment that he considered staying and making the Navy a career. He stated, "I found out that I could gain more in a short period of time and possibly retire early and move on to another career within, ah, the age range 30, 40 years old." Thus, he decided he would stay and serve 20 years. Even at the time he decided to stay and complete the minimum requirement to retire with full benefits, he had not considered that he would be selected for Chief.

When asked if there were any steps in the promotion process that he considered more difficult than others, he pointed to selection limits that existed within his line of work:

> Other than being in a rate at the time that was closed, the promotions were very close. At the time, during several cycles, no PCs [postal clerks] was promoted and I think I took that as a challenge because I was told that I'd never make Chief in that rate ... never make second [class petty officer] as far as that

goes. I took it as a challenge and, I worked harder to achieve that goal.... Basically, I just stuck with it. I knew eventually that it would change ... that it would open up down the road. Some people got impatient. I just stuck with it and that's the way I overcame the obstacle.

Additionally, he discussed how he was impacted by those who told him that he would make Chief:

It just made me work harder and like I said, I just took it as a challenge to not make it to prove them wrong, but to ah, show others that it could be done if they put their mind and heart to it and work toward it anything is possible. So I made it possible.

Chief Carter far exceeded his initial expectation of achieving the rank of third-class petty officer. I asked him if the challenges he faced changed as he progressed up the ranks toward Chief. He stated that they did:

Yes. The challenges, ah, changed somewhat ah the type of duty stations that you need to get promoted and those duty stations were then filled by other people that were trying to achieve the same goals that I was trying to achieve. So, ah, getting me the right stations ... geographical stations and positions became a challenge down the road because everyone wanted to get promoted and knew that we had to have this specific billet in order to get promoted.

The challenges he identified tended to involve the stated and accepted requirements for promotion to these higher levels. Up until this point, there had been no discussion of externally constructed barriers. When asked if he ever thought others constructed barriers for him, he replied,

Yea. I think at the middle, latter part of my career, I started to, ah, feel the pressure. People ... senior people placing obstacles in my way to try to stop me from being promoted, for whatever reason. Some of 'em — one in particular — was not putting me in various positions to be promoted. Other positions ... other times was writing evals in a manner to where they knew the wording in the evals would stop me from being promoted. It was different things ... different tactics.

I asked him how being placed in certain positions may affect one's promotion opportunities. He explained,

Well, you had to demonstrate leadership and other characteristics of leadership in order for them to properly grade you in that category. And if you're not in a leadership position or if you don't have that specific, ah, job position you can't be graded and you can't be ... you can't be graded in that position if you can't be put into it. Therefore, when it comes down to eval time, you, you're scored lower because you're not in that actual position.

Following up on his points, I asked if he thought this was a way of affecting promotions that exists outside the formal requirements. He responded,

> I could go along with that. But on the other hand, you know, you only have certain positions within a department/division ... that one can get in ... so if that's the case and someone is already filling that position, you either have to wait until that individual's out or you try to do other things to make up for that. Or either you transfer out to a position that ... where you can fill.

Because his earlier comments seem to suggest that he believed his military superiors were deliberately not assigning him to positions that he needed for advancement, I asked him for clarification on this point. When asked if he thought he was deliberately denied positions that he needed for promotions, he responded,

> Yea, I felt that ... however, the individual who was placing [me] in that position felt that I could be better utilized in that position because, one, the other guys didn't want it and I was the only one that was maybe there to possibly take it ... was one excuse that was given. Another excuse that was given was that this guy has been in this position for X amount of months and years, and although he's not properly doing the job, we just can't, you know, remove him without some type of hiccup.

Although he faced challenges, this participant stated that he never thought of quitting. He explained why:

> No. To be honest, I never thought of quitting I always thought, about the end result and I always thought that if I didn't get it, it wasn't meant for me to have and, ah, there was other things down the road. So I believed in [the adage that] a quitter never wins. So I just kept going [and] down the road, I was rewarded.

This reward culminated in his being promoted to the rank of Chief. This achievement is often viewed as a highlight of many enlisted Navy personnel's careers. It was an important milestone for him as well. He discussed how it felt when he learned he had been selected for Chief:

> Well, I made it fairly early and, ah, it was like a load being lifted off my shoulder I felt that the journey was over. I achieved something that a lot of people was ... hadn't achieved and was working hard. I just felt like it was a load being lifted off. A sense of accomplishment.

I asked Chief Carter if, after having been selected for Chief, he retained any residual negative feelings. He responded, "Not really. I think a lot of my negative feelings came once I made Chief and, and I think that's when more blatant ... to me how the system was run and who ran it." I asked him to explain what he meant. He added,

> Prime example, one duty station that I was in, I was filling an E-9 billet and with that title, being an E-7 going up for E-8, was almost a shoo-in. Ah,

but when the eval was written, it was watered down. It didn't say that this guy was filling an E-9 billet. It said, "This guy was filling a higher billet," which is, you know, when you look at that, it paints two different stories.

I asked him to elaborate on what he meant when he mentioned the "system" and "who ran it." He continued,

Well, you got your supervisors there, and, you know, that regardless of what you know and what you do, if this individual has some type of bad feeling toward you for whatever reason, [for example] he feels you should be doing something else. When it comes down to evaluation time, you, you know regardless of what your job is ... how many people you got working for you, it's always the, ah, close-to-the-throne syndrome. What I mean by that is that, an individual could be a slacker or whomever, if he's close to the individual that's doing the write-up, well it's obvious that that individual's gonna get a better write-up, regardless of what type of work you're doing at the time.

Our conversation then shifted to what he felt he had accomplished while on active duty and those accomplishments that were sources of pride for him. He discussed some specific lessons that he passed on to junior sailors that he considered an important accomplishment:

Well, ah, I tried to teach guys that you know, be a good leader regardless of what's going on be honest to your troops; let 'em know the good and the bad. Also, some of the decisions that, ah, you may have to put down, although some of 'em you may not agree with, you stress that in private, but when it's time to put it out, you've got to get 100% behind it and not say that, "Hey, this is what my division officer wants." You've got to go with "This is what I want" and go forward with it.

He proceeded to discuss some things of which he was particularly proud. As he did when discussing his accomplishments, he focused this discussion mainly on his impact on junior sailors:

Helping troops get promoted; seeing 'em progress ... seeing several of 'em go on up to officers, warrant officers, ah, go higher basically than what I did. I like to see 'em advance and prove themselves. And if they didn't stay in the military, I like to see 'em take something back with 'em that would assist them in the civilian sector with being a good leader.

In accomplishing the things he believes he accomplished in helping junior sailors, Chief Carter believes he made a long-term difference. As he put it, "I think so. Granted [a] lot of these kids come from single parents. Some didn't have a, a male figure in their life to sort of steer 'em and I think I made a difference in a lot of their life to [do] much better themselves." However, while he believed he accomplished some important thing and made a long-term difference, he does not believe he was properly rewarded. I asked him about this and he responded,

> No I don't feel like I was rewarded properly. Ah, but you know, who am I to say? I'm not the one that's, you know, doing the rewarding. Sometimes you always feel you should get more than what you got, but another person my have a different look at it. So, ah, I don't try ... [I] try not to dwell on that. I just, you know, try to keep a positive outlook on, on everything and if you think negative about things they become negative so.... Ah, I guess that's life.

Although he feels he accomplished much by helping to develop junior sailors, he did cite two things that he wishes he had been able to accomplish. He stated that he wishes he had promoted higher in the system and that he had completed his college degree. Given the opportunity to do it over, he stated that he would place more emphasis on those two goals.

We then shifted our conversation to the subject of mentorship. This participant indicated his view that mentorship is important to career development and that the Navy was right to implement a formal mentorship program. Discussing the Navy's mentorship program, he stated,

> I think it's a good thing. I think, ah, everybody needs someone else's view of things. Someone who's already been through it or going through it probably can better guide you through some of the obstacles. I think it's a good thing. I probably think they probably should have incorporated it much sooner because you have the young kids coming in, like I said, that had single parents and didn't have anyone else they can go to, they could steer 'em and sort of talk to 'em. So yea, it's a good thing.

Chief Carter himself did not have a formal mentor as he was coming up through the ranks, and by the time the formal mentorship program was incorporated he was too far along in his career to benefit from such a program. As he articulated it,

> No I didn't ... I felt at that point I was on the downswing of my career, I knew that I was getting out. Ah, I don't even think at that point a mentor would have done me any good. Maybe I was wrong; maybe not, but I was on the downswing. I knew I was getting out. I wasn't going any further so I didn't bother with it.

While he felt that the formal mentorship program was incorporated too late to impact his career, he did acknowledge receiving guidance from more senior sailors as he was progressing through the ranks. He noted that terms such as "mentor" were not used to refer to those senior personnel who provided guidance. As he put it, they were "just somebody ... [that]

... an individual ... would go to and talk over things. That [person] was my Chief. I, ah, I got guidance from him and he didn't steer me wrong."

He stated that he felt that this person did a good job in serving his needs because he "knew how the system worked and how the promotion things would work and what to write down and how to write it down. So he done me well." In comparing the mentorship he received with that received by White sailors, he added,

> Ah, I really, I really can assume. I really don't know I think they probably [were] more pampered than the minority sailors and they was given more opportunities to advance. Ah, I think they were placed probably in some of these positions to get advanced. So that's my assumptions of that.

When discussing informal settings often cited as opportunities for the transfer of information, he added,

> Ah, yea, I was invited [but] I didn't go. I don't think [a] lot of the information on being promoted was given there. I think the general information was given in forums like that, but I think a lot of the other information probably was given under the table, like any other place.... You know, you may tell your guys, "Okay, you know this is the place you wanna be. This is the best spot for you to get promoted. This is where you should request to go ... this is where I'm gonna put you. Just do whatever and we'll make sure you make it." And so on and so forth.

This participant seemed careful not to overemphasize the role race may have played in his advancement or differences that may have existed due to race. When asked if he recognized any differences in how the "under the table" information that he mentioned was transferred to Black sailors when compared to White sailors, he stated, "Ah, I really don't know. I really can't honestly answer that question. Like I said, I probably could assume something, but I can't...." Similarly, he was reluctant to state that race had played any role in his advancement:

> Ah, I don't think race had that much to do with me being promoted. I think it was the individual's own perception that may have held me from being promoted. It wasn't ... I don't know what was going through ... maybe it was race. Maybe not. It probably had something to do with it.

While he believed the military was more merit-based than many nonmilitary organizations, he did not believe the military had achieved a pure meritocracy. I asked him if he could recall any specific times when race may have been used in making career decisions. He responded,

> In one of my commands I felt that the captain, one of the captains that I worked for, ah, he gave — it was a Black guy that was there prior to me — and

he caught pure hell there with him and when I got there, I caught some of the same. However, we had the most responsibility within the department. But we were always ranked much lower than our counterparts, either White or Black or someone that was close to him ... they were ranked much higher.

He stated that he felt that sometimes these actions were based on race and sometimes they were based on what he referred to as "close-to-the throne syndrome." In defining this term, he stated,

> So I guess who's closest to him, who he knows the best, who he liked, the demeanor, or someone who kissed up to him, someone, you know, who laughed at his corny jokes. Ah, I don't know. They ... you know, people have their own way of choosing who gets the highest, evals and I don't think job responsibilities is one of 'em.

He was very clear in his belief that race had also been a positive factor in his career advancement. He explained the positive experiences he had with race in the following example:

> Yea, guys that I worked for that, you know, basically said, "this is where you need to be. This is what you got to do if you wanna go there. I'll put you there." Ah, it's been a little of both. You know, you got to mix things. But, you know, essentially I was in control of that. I could have, maybe made a stink about it, but I don't know. That's just the way life goes.

He added that when it came to issues such as training, race had no impact and that he believed training was "given to everybody equally, across the board." He asserted that, overall, race did not have much of an impact. We concluded the discussion with his characterization of the overall impact race has had on his career:

> I would say minimal. I wouldn't say a great role. I think I had some of the, some of the same opportunities others had ... some of the White counterparts had. Did I take advantage of them? Yes. Maybe no. Could I have? Probably yes. So I don't think that was too much of a hindrance.

Senior Chief Evanston

Senior Chief Evanston stated that he had no intentions of enlisting in the Navy. Prior to the Navy, he attended Hampton Institute in Virginia and his family could not afford to continue financing his education. He also stated that he enjoyed travel and decided that joining the Navy would be one way to fulfill his desire to travel while also providing a means of getting an education. Although his father had served 4 years in the Navy, this was not a primary impetus for Senior Chief Evanston to join. He stated, "He did 4 years, there were some good points and some bad points but I always had my sense that I'm not my dad and his reality was not my reality." In the end, he and his brother enlisted in the Navy one week apart.

Senior Chief Evanston stated that when he enlisted, he had no intention of pursuing a career. According to him, "I was gonna stay in the Navy long enough to get a degree and get out. And like I said, also satisfy my desire to travel and see the world. After being in the Navy for a while...my first 4 years in the Navy was fun. I really enjoyed it. I really got a kick out of what I was doing." He stated that after his first enlistment, "I saw no reason why not to further my career. At one point.... okay, well let me put it this way, after my first enlistment I really said, 'yea, this is gonna be pretty cool. I like this. I can see myself becoming a Chief or Chief Warrant Officer.'" However, he wanted to be a hands-on technician and that led to his decision to strive to become a Chief. In his own words,

> I really had no desire, even though there was a lot of pressure on me many years down the road, around my 10-year mark, from my command to become an officer. And in one situation I actually was accepted and I turned it down. And the only reason why I did it was because my CO pretty much told me I had to do it. And I never wanted to do what the officers did. I never cared about the prestige and I never cared about the title. All I cared about was learning my trade, learning what ... doing what I wanted to do and being in the trenches or mentoring other people to do what we were doing. I wanted to be a hands-on administrator in the electronics field. And I saw what the officers did that supervised me. They were more knife and fork, political ... entities and I didn't want anything to do with that.

Senior Chief Evanston stated that he found promotions to come easy. However, he did identify what he perceived to be barriers. He discussed a scenario that he said occurred in 1982 when he came face-to-face with overt racism:

> And so what I did was I cross-decked to another ship and the other ship is when I had a heavy dose of "What the hell am I doing here." The ship that ah, the ship had came from San Diego and, ah, when I got onboard the ship, I was standing before my Division Officer ... had me standing at attention for well over 45 minutes and finally I cleared my throat. And I knew right away I was in for an issue here. There was something wrong here. And the division officer looked up to me, looked up at me and said "You know, your kind [is] not supposed to be a electronics technician. Your kind is supposed to be either a boatswains mate, or a MS and if it's the last thing I do I will see to it that that's what you become."

He stated that he was harassed by other sailors throughout much of his stay on the ship. He also stated that he later learned that this ship had a formal chapter of the KKK and that his division officer was a member. However, he stated that once the commanding officer learned of this, he removed the members from the ship. I asked him why he stayed after all he had endured. He responded,

> My dad said to me, "You know, let me tell you something. The very reason that, just by the fact that they wanted you to get out, is reason enough for you to stay in. If you liked it and you liked what was going on, you liked what it was all about and you let people dictate how you control your life or how you choose your destiny, then they've won and you've lost."

He said he stayed in because of his father's comments and because of the encouragement he received from his commanding officer. He added that he coped with his challenges by being resilient. He explained,

> I had to be resilient. And I need to expand on that. It's whenever, and I've carried this with me and because the Navy showed me this so well, I've carried this always through my present.... So in other words, when I ran into that proverbial brick wall, the brick wall would never stop me ... if I could, I would go around it. If I couldn't, I would go over it. If I had to, I dug [under] it and in some cases I went right through it. But the brick wall was never a permanent obstacle. I was always resilient.

Senior Chief Evanston stayed in the Navy and was eventually promoted to Chief. I asked him how it felt to be selected for that rank. He offered an enthusiastic response:

> That was one of the crowning highlights of my military career. You know, I don't think there's any other place on this planet that transcends from one phase to another so absolutely as being a Chief in the Navy. You know, as a first-class petty officer, you know, it's like, yea okay. Then as a Chief, it's like, "What do you think, Chief." My word was like, it was absolute. You know, when they say that the Chief is truly the backbone of the Navy, that is an understatement. It's like, I'm just gonna hold this in play. The level of respect because of that uniform is, was unbelievable ... people [who] would question what you say, wouldn't anymore simply because you're a Chief. It was a big sense of accomplishment. I'd say that of all the things that I did accomplish in the Navy, that was the biggest. So there you go. That was it right there. That was my biggest sense of accomplishment in the Navy, from a career standpoint.

I then asked him if, after what he endured in the Navy, he retained any negative feelings. He responded as follows:

> Well, you know what. This is the way I look at it. You take experience and you catalog it. You catalog it so that you always have that remembrance to go

3. Participants' Profiles   57

to, to help you with the situation that's happening in the present. That's what it's there for. You know, what I did learn to do is when I would catalog it, I would catalog it through a filter and that filter was to remove any hate and any negativity that would drag me down as a person. Because the people that hated me, did not hate me because they knew me. They hated me because they were ignorant, because they were afraid, because they didn't understand. And, when you keep that in that context, you just realize that all I have to do now is become more aware.

He continued,

I've talked to a lot of brothers that all they cried about [was] "Man the Navy's f'd up. Man oh man, I can't wait to get out the Navy, blah, blah, blah, blah, blah, blah." I said, "Well, you know, you're complaining, but what are you doing about it?"

As our conversation continued, I asked him to talk about what he considers to be his most significant accomplishment as a Chief. He stated,

I would have to say, the brothers that I touched. That, that to me, is by far the most important thing. The brothers that I touched. Especially the ones that were on a downward spiral and I was able to bring them within my fold and I was able to mentor them and get them to understand that, that you have more control over your destiny than you think and while you're here and alive now, make the best of it and have that kind of mindset. I was able to turn around some really negative brothers and make it happen for them. And I think that the fact that I was a Chief, as opposed to a first class or second class, that automatic respect that you get from being a Chief gave me an edge as far as having them listen to what I had to say and point them in the right direction. It would definitely have to be helping the brothers that, that you know, was letting the system really, you know, take 'em out of their element. I think that was by far the most significant thing. I'm thinking about one person in particular. He reminded me of me so much when I was a mess crank. You know, and how even to this day him and I, we're still partners. We still communicate.

I asked him what he meant by "brothers" and he responded,

I mean African Americans. I've helped, now, now, I've helped lots of people that worked under me. I had this kid, this White kid, he's a rocker, he was a rocker from L.A. I mean he was one of those heavy metal kind of kids and he just hated everybody. And he just joined [the] Navy just to get away from the element ... there was a lot of heat where he was at. The Navy was just a way for him to escape, and, ah he worked in my calibration facility. And I was able to turn him around. And he became a stellar, stellar Petty Officer. You know, I was able to touch him. He was a good kid. I knew that. I saw past all the crap and saw that this kid was a good kid and I worked with this kid. And so, I didn't touch just Blacks, but I felt a lot better, I felt a lot more accomplishment when getting through to the Blacks simply because we had so much more going against us in the military that we needed an edge. We definitely needed an edge, you know. And whether that edge was internal or external, we did need it. It was no question about it. I definitely was not treated as an equal in a lot of sectors. Then in other sectors I was. So there were two sides to that. You know, I've worked in the commands where you know they really treated, you know, dealt with me based on my character more than anything else.

I asked Senior Chief Evanston if there were any things that he wishes he had accomplished but which he did not and he responded, "No. I pretty much did what I wanted to do." I then asked, if he had an opportunity to start his career over again, would he do anything differently. He responded,

I'll be honest with you, nobody wants adversity. I mean, albeit adversity in a lot of life does develop character, but, you know, who wants to go.... I wouldn't want to wish that crap on anybody. The stuff that I went through on my first command ... the stuff that I went through with the other.... I mean, I would rather not go through the stuff that I went through. You know, the negative stuff. Who wants.... I mean, if I could do it again without some of this crap, I would. But at the same time, like I told you, I look at it like this: This was the path my life that, that my life took. No matter what the path is, I have to have enough insight to pull some knowledge outta that and take that knowledge with me and let it help me somewhere down the road. You know, where I catalog it in my hard drive in my brain and have the ability to pull that resource out when I need to, to help me make wise decisions in the future.

My conversation with Senior Chief Evanston then shifted to a discussion of mentorship. He stated that he never had any formal mentors when he was in the Navy and that he had never heard of the Navy's formal mentorship program. However, he did have informal mentors. He discussed his relationship with his mentors and the role they played in his career:

Informal mentors? Yea, I had plenty of those. I'd sit down and play bid-wiz and play dominos with warrant officers and other officers and other Chief Petty Officers and first classes and most of these people were senior to me at any given point in time. And they were chock full of knowledge. They were chock full of support. They, they really educated me on the ropes. On how to deal with a lot of situations. You know, they give you this information, you take that information. You digest it. You process it and you decide whether this.... "I'll use this piece" or "I don't use that piece." As time goes on, and you learn to be a good listener, you learn. You become more efficient at processing that data and filtering out the stuff that's not of any real value or maybe of value at another time and then the information that's really of value to you at that time. And, and yea I've learned a lot. Even to this day, I still learn a lot from people that have more experience than me in the things that they do. I like to think that this is something that will go on for the rest of my life.

When I asked him to discuss the quality of his mentors he offered an interesting perspective:

> The Whites nor the Black, neither one was better than the other and I'll tell you why. Now, they all had their own place and value. Because the Black mentors gave me information that was necessary for me as a Black man to make good judgments in tough situations. Okay. And that was the perspective from a Black point of view. The White mentors gave me a different perspective. They gave me the perspective inside the White man's head. And they gave me perspective from how the guys, the White guy that's not, that does not have my best interest and value, how he's thinking. They gave it to me honestly and ah objectively. And it was, it was invaluable because I'm not White. I don't live a White lifestyle. I was born a Black man, always will be a Black man. I, even though I've lived in a multicultural environment, I can't think like a White person no more than a White person can really think like me because we don't live the same experiences. But the White mentors in my life gave me a different point of view, a point of view that a Black man just couldn't give me. And those points of view educated me that much more.

He then offered his view of how the mentorship Whites received compares to that received by Black sailors. He stated, "From the outside looking in, I think that the Whites that were receptive to being mentored had access to more resources than we did." I asked him to elaborate and he explained,

> Because the people, some people who were mentoring the Whites were not mentoring the Blacks. And whether we like it or not, we don't run the military. And when I say run the military, I'm talking about the essence of the military. We run parts of it. We have control over parts of it. You know, we have generals. I mean we've gone all the way up the chain. But it's still, the core group, the core essence of the Navy is still White. And the ones who hold the most power and the most control over what's going on in the Navy — and I'm just using the Navy 'cause that's where I was — is still White. So if you fall under that type of mentorship you can go farther faster easier if you're a quick learner. Does that make sense to you? Do you understand what I mean? So, whereas I might, as I go up that chain of command, as I progress in life somewhere along the line in the Navy, I'm gonna run into a road block that's gonna try to hamper me, that's gonna wanna suppress me simply because I'm an African American. Now, bear in mind, some kind, some White person might run into a similar roadblock because he's Italian. And this Irish commander has a thing against Italians. But that's a lot more, that's more secular than our situation. If you understand what I mean. That, that is more finite as opposed to how it is as far as African Americans are concerned. Because African Ameri-

can, we ... it just spans all the way across the board with us; whereas here, it's more item per item. There's an exception here and there. And ... yea, there's more roadblocks for us going up that chain. Whereas, anybody [who] wants to cultivate and turn this young White man or White woman who has the potential to become a general definitely has a less arduous trail ... than I or African Americans would or most minorities for that matter.

While he believed that White sailors had access to more effective mentorship, he left no doubt that he believed his competence was equal to that of his White colleagues and that it was accepted as such:

See, the one thing that really got me through a lot was because I was so damn good at my field. I mean, it became ... in some cases I was very cocky about the fact that I was so good at what I did. And I exuded confidence. When it came to my field, I always felt I was second to no one. That was, I believe, one of my edges. So no matter how much anybody disliked me or no matter what kind of crap I went through, in very few situations did anybody challenge my expertise in what I did. I studied my butt off. I always did my research. I always made a point that when I opened my mouth, I knew what the hell I was talking about and that I was right.... Chiefs inherently, I think, to a certain degree are cocky. You know, there's cockiness about us. You know, because you don't just get to be a Chief. In most cases than not, some do squeak through, granted, some do, their timing was right [and] they managed to squeak through. But that's really the exception. Most of the Chiefs I've met really know their job. They know what they're doing. There is a small percentage that is flakes, but not, not usually. The Chief's position is extremely competitive.

We then shifted our conversation to discuss his views regarding the military's claim of meritocracy. When asked whether he believes the Navy has created a meritocracy, he responded, "It's a combination. It's a hodgepodge of both. It is based on meritocracy but at the same time you do run into barriers." When asked if those barriers were mainly associated with race, he responded,

Yes. No question about it. No question about it. Yes. Yes it is. You can go in a command where it's strictly based on your merit. You know, you can actually go [in] a command where ... where the division officer ... believes in meritocracy ... he's basing it on your merit. But your LPO doesn't. You know. So who's evaluating you? The division officer or the LPO? So if you don't have the whereforwits to know to, to, mind you go up the chain of command and get to the one that, that is really judging you fairly, is going to judge you fairly, you're, you're ended. You've reached a block, you, you're obscured. So, so yea, I think it's both. I was at a command where the CO really didn't care what the heck was going on with me.... He didn't put any value into it whereas the next CO, he very much believed in the character of the individual, and, and you know and what was going on, you know. I just really depends on who you're dealing with and when.

He subsequently added,

> You know. And I think, yea, that is the essence of the military. That's what it's supposed to be ... that's what they claim, and like I said, to a certain degree it's true. But that system, you have to understand, that system, all things being equal, would work, but there's one factor in that that makes it imperfect, and that's people. Everybody thinks about things differently. People with their own agendas, you know hidden agendas; people with their own prejudices; people with their partiality; you know, those things always play a factor ... not always play a factor, but they play a factor in a lot of cases. And as long as they do, that form of recognition is always going to be flawed. Because that doesn't take into account the human factor.

Senior Chief Gregg

Like many others, Senior Chief Gregg did not enlist in the Navy with the intention of staying for an entire career. He stated that his primary reason for enlisting in the Navy is because his father had been a Navy man. Speaking of his father, Senior Chief Gregg stated, "he always came back telling U.S. Navy stories when I was growing up so that's what I always wanted to do." Once he enlisted, rather than deciding to stay for a defined period of time, he said he "just took it in increments" because he did not know what it was all about. Then he added, "You know, and after I hit a certain point, like when I hit that ... 'cause I reenlisted twice and every time I reenlisted they gave me $16,000 as a bonus because of the job I had. And then when I reenlisted and it took me to the 12-year mark and it ended, I'm like, 'well, I might as well stay for another 8. 'Cause it's not hard.'"

I asked him if he had given any consideration to how far he might rise in the Navy's hierarchy. He seemed to have some well-defined goals fairly early on in his career. He stated, "I always wanted to ... I wanted to get to E-9. I wanted to get to that Master Chief rank. And then once I made E-8, and the things they were telling me I needed to get to E-9, I was like, I'm not doing that." He then explained what some of those things were:

> Yea. Well one of the things was the people in the air traffic control community, first of all they were upset when I left the air traffic control community to become an Equal Opportunity Advisor. They were upset about that. When I left ... when I told them I wanted to leave to do something else, and I was a Chief then, they told me "Well, you can go if you want to but you will never make E-8." You know, like they had the power to stop it. And, ah, pretty

much I believe they did. They had, they had ins and outs to do things like that, I believe. You know, they could talk to somebody on the board, who knew somebody else and things like that to go, "Okay, when you get to this guy's record, you know I just want you to know that he's deserting us." I said, "Well, screw you." I went to the job anyway because I didn't want to work with people that had that kind of philosophy. And when I made E-8 anyway, despite them, then they told me, "Well, if you wanna make E-9, you have to come back to being an air traffic controller and you have to go to an aircraft carrier." I said, "Number one, I don't want to go to an aircraft carrier. Number two, I don't wanna be an air traffic controller anymore. So you can keep it. I'll just get out."

Although this participant did not know how long he would stay in the Navy, he did seem to know that he wanted to rise up the rank structure. He eventually rose to the level of Senior Chief. I asked him if there were any steps along the way that he found more difficult than others. He recounted his experiences:

Well, the thing was, for me, when I was on my first ship it was a command ... and I've known for some time that it was an anomaly because every place I went thereafter, it wasn't like this. When I was on my first ship there were, there were like eight Blacks on the ship ... eight Black males on the ship. And the leading guy was a Senior Chief who became a Master Chief. And he was a Black guy also. So I kinda had him to look over me. But the thing about the Navy for me is I always did a good job. Doing a good job there just came easy to me. And I was always ... and the brothers who were in there with me, they always worked hard also. So the, the Black Master Chief, he always made sure I was on the right path and doing the right thing. So I had a good mentor ... in my early years ... I was just, you know, an E-4 ... E-3, E-4 up like that. But there were times when I knew that it all depends on whether or not your leadership liked you. If they liked you, you were good to go. If they didn't like you, they could hold you up. Now like I was talking about we were on the ship, you know we had eight brothers on the ship, I was an E-3 at the time when I got to the ship. There were two other brothers there who were E-6s. And as an E-3, I went up through the ranks and I passed both of them. They both had to retire [as] E-6s because they wasn't very well liked you know. And I have, I don't know if you wanna call it assimilation or whatever, but I have the ability to do whatever it takes and everybody just liked the way I did business, you know.

I asked him if the others who did not succeed in becoming Chief have poor performance. He stated that he believed they worked hard but that he believed "They had more attitude. Or you know they found things that they wanted to do and that's what they did." He added, "You know, and a lot of them came from, actually both of these E-6s, they came from the South. So they didn't have a good, ah, they didn't like White people too much. So they had issues with White people and they voiced that."

While he stated that many of the African American men with whom he worked were never selected for Chief, Senior Chief Gregg was. I asked him how it felt to achieve this rank. He responded,

> When I made Chief, [I was] very proud. Even more so I knew my father was going to be very proud. As a person who grew up into a, I mean who was a part of a very racist Navy when he came up. You know, "you're Black, this is your job — cook. You're Black, this is your job — steward." That's it. So he was proud to see his sons have jobs like air traffic controller and electronic technician and to see both his sons become Chief. I was very proud of that. Especially as an air traffic controller because there were not very many air traffic controllers, period.

After he discussed how he felt when he was selected for Chief, I asked him if he had encountered any barriers as he ascended the rank structure. He responded,

> Oh yea. Actually the hardest time I had was when I actually made Chief. Once I actually put the Chief's uniform on that's when I ran into all craziness. Especially on the ship, when the, ah, the Chief who was there, he was getting ready to leave and the commander that he worked for — I can't straight up say he didn't like Blacks because ... but I can straight up say he didn't like women — so to me I could say, if you were a minority, he didn't like you. So he stood right next to me, when the guy was getting ready to leave, me and the leaving Chief, he was leaving and the commander stood right there in front of both of us and said [to him], "Please don't go. I will do whatever it takes for you to stay here." You know, "I need you to be here. What are we going to do without you." And I'm standing right there. God damn. I mean you have that little faith in me and I hadn't been doing a bad job since I been there. You know, this wasn't my first ship, so I knew what I had to do. But he was just, "Don't do it." So anytime, you know, some serious situation came up, he just tried to just bowl me over, "We're going to do it this way." I'm like "Commander, the book says we have to do it this way; We're gonna do it this way." You know, he'd say, "Are you arguing with me?" "No sir, I'm not arguing with you. We'll do it your way." Until, ah, we came to heads one day when it just became real ugly when I told him, "I don't give a damn what you do to me after I'm doing with this job, but I'm gonna do it this way ... whether you like it or not."

A commander is a senior officer in most Navy organizations. I asked Senior Chief Gregg how his approach to dealing with this commander worked out. He offered a detailed response:

> Well, it worked out fine for me, because what it was is a situation where, you know, we've gotta control an airplane. I'm in charge of all the airplanes that's in the sky controlling them by radar and all the radars went out and so we've got 20 some airplanes in the air and nobody could see anyone of 'em and

then the radios went out. Now you've got 20 airplanes in the air, no radar, no radio and it's dark outside. And my boss, she's sitting right behind me as I'm doing this and she's saying, and she's talking to the commander on the phone and the commander is telling her to "do this, and do this, and do this." And she looked at me and said, "Chief, the commander said do this, do this, do this." I said, "We're not going to do that. This is what we're going to do." And I said, "You need to tell the commander this is what we're going to do." And she kinda like freaked out. She got ulcers from him. She goes, "I don't think I can tell him that." I said, "Well, you need to tell him that." And then she told him. Soon as she told him that, he comes—'cause he's right next door—he comes busting through the door, and you've got a room full of E-3s up to E-5s, E-6s all in there right there, 20 of 'em in the room and he comes running right up to my face blathering at the mouth, "You will do what I tell you and you will do this, this, this, and this and you...." [Laughter] In the whole room, nobody is even looking up. Everybody is like, "Oh my God." I said, "Commander, what you want to do is not safe and is illegal. I know exactly what this book says; I know exactly what I'm doing. As a matter of fact, this is not the first time I've done this. What I'm gonna do is this, this, this, this, this, this, this. I recommend that you call the captain and let him know that this is what the deal is." And he just looked at me. And he turned around and walked away. He was like, "You expect me to tell the captain that? You expect...?" "Sir, you don't have to tell the captain anything, but this is what I'm gonna do." And he went storming outta there. And I told those controllers ... those controllers looked at me just like, "Chief, oh man you've got big *cojones*." And we did it, all those airplanes got home safe. Three of those controllers got the, eh, I forget what the medals are called. But three of the controllers got medals for the job they did during the recovery, bringing those airplanes down, because it was a messed up situation. From that point on, he left me alone. He never said anything to me; he just concentrated his efforts on the women. You know, just being negative toward them. But he left me alone. From that point on he was like, we were cool. You know, he could joke with me now. Before, he wouldn't. You know, now he wanna joke with me. Now I'm his boy. To me I was like, "Nah, I have no respect for you."

As he continued discussing the obstacles he believes he had to overcome, he added:

He was an anomaly. He was just a walking anomaly. A ... everything that I was ... it was always a "show me you can do it first and then I'll have trust in you." Instead of like "This is your job. Go ahead and do it," it was like "this is your job, I wanted to see if you can do it first. And then once you do it and do it well, then, eh, then everything is fine." But every time I was put in those positions of doing it, I did it and I did it well and that just helped me move up the ranks. You know I got put ... I was the leading Petty Officer as an E-6. As a junior E-6 I was put in that position above E-6s who were senior to me. The Navy just came easy to me. I just thought it was easy. I just met people who were full of themselves when I got to the Chiefs' ranks. You know, like the guys who told me "you will never make E-8 if you leave us." ... I'm like

"Okay, so what are you going to do to stop me from making E-8." You know, I don't know if they did anything. But I know, you know, all my time in the Navy I had people say "No you're not gonna make Chief. I know somebody on the board." You know, and I've seen a lot of people — a lot of Blacks — who just didn't make it because of words like that: "You're not gonna make it."

Although Senior Chief Gregg stated earlier in the conversation that he liked the Navy and found it easy to do well throughout his career, he cited several incidents that he considered obstacles that he had to overcome. In addition to the ones above, he discussed the following situation where his commander would not allow him to perform the task with which he was charged and for which he was trained:

> I had to leave that place because I would never get any respect from him and I firmly believe it was because of race. This guy would just, he would tell me things in my face, "Oh no, you're doing fine." You know, we went to a, a briefing. When I was in Point Mugu I was in charge of the control tower, so all the airplanes that fly, visually I'm in charge of the tower. I would have to go brief the pilots and he would come with me to brief the pilots. He wasn't even supposed to be there. But then he was there. So I told 'em, Okay, this is what we're going to talk about, this is this, this is this, this is that. I told 'em about whatever is going on at the time. And I'd say, "What questions do you have for me?" The first person that would raise their hand, I'd go, "Okay go ahead, Lieutenant." He'd ask me a question. As soon as I opened my mouth my division officer answered the question. Somebody else asked another question. He answered that question too. He answered all the questions. I got nothing. I didn't answer one single question. I'm like, "What am I, his bodyguard standing there?" That's what it felt like. And I was like, I had never felt more inadequate. 'Cause I know they were looking at me awful, like "Why are you standing up here, Chief, if you're not going to answer any of these questions?" I was thinking like, you know what, I'm not putting up with that. The very next day I was waiting at his office for him to come to work. When he got to work, I said, "Sir, you mind if we have a talk?" [He said] "Sure. Come on in the office." [I] went into his office. I said, ah, "I didn't understand what was going on yesterday." I said, "I felt like you had no confidence, no faith in my knowledge, or my ability to answer any of these questions the officers asked because you answered all of them." He just looked at me and went "No, no, no, no, no, no, I believe in, no, no, it's nothing like that, no, no, no. You're doing fine, da, da, da." And I'm like Why didn't I get a chance to answer any of those questions? [He said] "I didn't realize I was doing that." I said "Okay, that's fine." I just left it at that. You know, but him and the other Chiefs there — 'Cause I was the only Black Chief there — they were just such poor leaders. I was just like, "You know what, this place is driving me crazy. I don't even want to go to work." When I left, they said "Okay, we're gonna give you the Navy Achievement Medal when you leave." So I left there. I got to my new duty station, I'm like, "Okay, where's the medal? The medal is supposed to come." You know, the paper work was a little slow. It's supposed to come.

When I called back to Personnel, [I] said, "Hey I'm supposed to get a Navy Achievement Medal and I'm wondering what's the hold up? Is the write up wrong and had to be redone or something? What's going on?" He goes, "Oh no, maybe about like a month after you left they ... your division officer just pulled that medal." [Laughter] I said "really?" He said, "Oh yea, he came down here and did it himself. He just withdrew it." I said, "Wow." He couldn't do anything to my face, but behind my back this is what he did.

One response to significant barriers in the workplace is to stop trying to succeed. When I asked Senior Chief Gregg if he ever considered quitting, he was quick to state, "I wasn't giving up on the Navy. I just gave up on that place. I'm not giving up on the Navy because I've got, you know, 10 years to go, whatever, to retire and I'm gonna retire." Moreover, he stated that, in spite of the barriers, he retained no negative feelings. Explaining his views, he stated,

No. My feelings weren't negative. I just knew that it existed. I knew that racists existed. I'm not going to walk around being bitter about the way life is. Because number one, it doesn't help you. Number two, when you show that bitterness outwardly, then you'll get stuck wherever you are. You know, and I saw a lot, I met a lot of people who used that as an excuse whether it existed or not. [They would say], "Why are you trying to hold a brother down?" You know, sometimes these people worked with me. I'm like, "Ain't nobody holding you down. You ain't doing no work. [You] expect somebody to give you something. Nobody's trying to give you anything. You need to work for it."

Senior Chief Gregg clearly believes he made some significant accomplishments and he seemed proud of the impact he says he had on the lives "of a lot of young Black people." Describing his achievements, he stated,

I made a difference in the lives of a lot of young Black people. Especially once I made Chief and Senior Chief, I was somebody that — especially in the air traffic control world — I was somebody that a Black E-3 can go, "Wow, it can be done." And I would help them as long as they helped themselves. I would help them. You know, that means a lot to them to see that. They'd say, "How did you get to where you are?" [I'd say], "this is how I got to where I am. This is what you need to do." And like the Master Chief who mentored me when I was an E-3, I turned it around and did that for others. And it made me feel good to see them move up the ranks.

Although he believes he made a difference in the lives of a lot of young African American sailors, I was surprised to hear him say that his work did not make a long-term difference. He explained,

No. On an individual basis, maybe. Because a lot of those folks, I don't know where they are. But I think in the long-term, I think not. You know, I know I didn't change the minds of any White males ... when I confronted a lot of the White males and just issues of "I'm not doing that just because you say it. I don't care about that." You know, or try to teach them or show them that "your way is not the only way. You know, your way is just a way. Here goes some options, no matter what it is." But I knew if the majority agree with it, it would happen. They weren't happy. The only thing that would make them happy is when I left. You know, the main thing about me is I'm not going to do anything just because you said so. I'm definitely not going to do anything because you're the majority.

I then asked him if there were any things he wishes he had accomplished but did not and if, given the opportunity, he would do anything differently. He stated,

> That's a good question. I think the mark I left was individual marks and I wasn't trying to leave any kind of a legacy while I was there. You know 'cause pretty much then you get through the day, then you get through the day, [you say] what do I need to do for tomorrow? And I looked at it like that. I don't know [if I would do anything differently]. I don't know if I would ... talk to some of the people ... there's lots of people who had negative attitudes, you know, like my division officer, were people who were much senior to me. So a lot of complications I had, I dealt with them on my individual basis. But nothing where to the point where me reporting somebody or, you know, like when they took away that medal from me. I could have took it to another level. If I thought it was worth it. But sometimes like that, I just let some of the battles just go. I said, "Just forget it. It's not worth it."

He stated that if he had an opportunity to start over, he would confront some of those issues that he did not confront the first time. He stated, "I think I would've taken those battles on if I'd have known then what I knew toward the end of my career. Toward the end of my career, you know, once I went to DEOMI and got a lot of that knowledge, because after I got that knowledge, I'd take anybody on. I don't care what it is."

Our conversation then shifted to the topic of mentorship. I asked Senior Chief Gregg to discuss any experiences he had with mentorship as he progressed through the Navy ranks. He responded,

> I received mentorship from the ... it was definitely not from a program. I was a part of no mentorship program. What I got was what turned out to be mentorship was when I went to my first ship — the ship that had the eight Blacks — and I had the two E-6s there, they mentored me. You know, they showed me how to do things. And I also had the Black Master Chief. And then when I made Chief, I really had no mentorship and that's why I hated that place. I was at Point Mugu. I couldn't stand that place. Here I am a brand new Chief. And I would go to work, [and] as a Chief, I knew things were supposed to be different." But there was this female Senior Chief who was in charge and I'm, like, I'm getting nothing. I'm getting no guidance. I'm just,

> I'm just flowing around every day trying to figure out what I'm supposed to be doing. You know, with this division officer who doesn't give me any respect. And half the time I'd go sit in my office. I could go sit in my office all week and nobody would even know it. Not doing anything.

He described the quality of the mentorship he received as being effective because of the rank he achieved. Additionally, he viewed the mentorship to be "like big brother looking out for little brother. That's pretty much what it was like." He clearly appreciated the mentorship he received from these informal mentors. Discussing his feelings about the quality of the mentorship they provided, he stated,

> Yea. These are people very near ... this is, I'm talking about situations that were 20 years ago, when I met these guys. I still talk to these guys today. One of them I talked to today. These are people who do, who cared about me. They cared about me. Made sure I didn't get in trouble, do things like that. I was very fortunate to have those guys there. That's how ... actually, it may have changed my whole attitude about ... altering the course of my development while I was in the Navy. Because if I'd have went through this ship and there wasn't these Black guys there, these older Black guys there, who just, I mean as soon as I got there, they just sucked me right up. If they were not there, there really is no telling what my future would have been like in the Navy.

I then asked him to discuss his views of the mentorship White sailors received in the commands in which he served. He continued,

> I think they got it too. They did get that. You know, I'm just thinking about one ship. I know on one ship they didn't get that because the senior people were Black people. They got no more than anybody else got. But when I went to other ships, my other duty stations, no matter how you slice it, there was no mentorship no matter how you slice it, nothing formal anyway. Informally, yes. Informally, there was.... I'm not gonna call it mentorship. I'm just gonna call 'em hook-ups. Informally, lots and lots of hook-ups. "You're my boy. I'm gonna take care of you. I'm gonna give you the best job. I'm gonna put you in the best position, you know, where you'll be in the limelight; people will recognize who you are. You'll get noticed." That happened a lot. A lot of it was, in a particular case, say there's a Chief, a White Chief, if he likes ... these are his friends, so he's going to choose his friends, somebody he likes, "I want you to train up in this position because once you get qualified in this position, that's gonna bump you up above, ah, above a lot of other folks. Because of the procedure. I'm gonna put you in this position. I'm gonna put you in this position." A whole lot of people.

He proceeded to discuss a situation in one of his commands where he believed individuals were selected for training based on their race:

> I was the most senior Black person at one command and there were two or three junior White folks. And these other, all these other White folks were getting picked to train on the air traffic control equipment. A lot of the Black kids would come to me and say, "Hey, I don't know if you notice this, but I've been busting my butt studying. I've been busting my butt on this and this and they picked this person over me to do that." And I said, "Let me see what I can do." And I would talk to the Chief. I'd say, "Hey Chief, what's the deal? My man here was working hard and is he gonna get a shot?" And he'd go "Oh yea, yea, his time is coming. His time is coming." And I'd say "Okay, his time is coming." You know, I'd say "Okay. We'll see how that goes." And his time didn't come. You know, the next thing you know, we're not at sea any more and you can't train if you're not at sea. And it was over with and I looked at that situation and was like "That's messed up." So the guys ... you know, these three or four Black guys, you know they're junior but they're not getting a shot to do anything. And the only thing that turned things around was before we went on the next deployment, I was made the LPO, and in charge of all the radar stuff. So now that I'm in that position I can go and get them trained. I was doing my best not to do it by race. I'm definitely trying to do it by merit but I know these Black guys and I know how hard they worked and I know how they just got looked over. I made sure that they got their shot.

Discussing how those who socialized with Chiefs benefit from those associations, he added,

> You had the Chief who'd say, "I like you." You know and this is who the Chief goes out, they all go out drinking together. I mean, and this is, it's kinda crooked. Because for the most part, like on the ship, us Black guys, we all hung out together, period. You know, we'd go to whoever's house and that's where we'd go, and the White guys, they hung out together. You see, the White guys, when they hung out together they're hanging out with the Chief, you know, who has the pull.

He stated that the Black sailors and White sailors did not socialize outside of work. However, since the White sailors were out socializing with the Chiefs, he added "The power was with the White guys."

When I asked Senior Chief Gregg if he believed race has played a role in his own career, he had much to say:

> Ah, one of the things, I've heard and I know I prefer not to use the word "assimilate," it wasn't really an act of trying to assimilate. It's just I know what the job entails and I know how to do it and I do it well and I get recognized for it. Like I say, the Navy was always easy to me. I didn't see a lot of racism stopping me from doing the things I really wanted to do. I just went out and did it and more times than not, more times than not, I got recognized for it. What made me different was, have you ever, ah ... but it's the way I act at times. And I wanna ask you a question. Have you ever been in a situation — and I've been in these situations a whole bunch of times and I've been in these

situations probably more times than I realize because people aren't saying it to my face. But on occasions I do hear them to my face and I've heard it after I left the military. It was "You know what, you really don't act like a Black guy. You don't act Black. You're not like the rest of them." Or something to that effect. At which point I get seriously offended and then I guess I show them what they think I'm supposed to be acting like if I'm Black if they say something like that. I think a lot of times ... for me, the expectation.... White people is they have of Blacks is that you're not that intelligent. You're not that sharp, so just like those four ... three or four Black guys, it's only ... they may not be able to handle the job, so let's go ahead and give it to somebody else. So when they encounter somebody who is intelligent that is Black, it kinda ticks 'em, you know, ticks 'em off. You know, takes 'em off their game a little bit. On the other hand, it's hard to tell that person "You can't do this. You can't do that" when you prove it to them on a regular basis.... When you prove it to 'em so many times, they go "You're just like one of us." "No I'm not." I don't know if you've ever heard that before. To me when they say that, that's their way of saying "We accept you." You know "We'll accept you because you're kinda like our token Black. You're outspoken, we accept you because you speak intelligently and you don't say "wif" and you don't have a curse word coming out of my mouth all the time. But you know what, when I'm around my friends I be cursing and cussing and carrying on and doing whatever. But I know that when I go to work, I cannot do that. What happens is, unfortunately, a lot of Blacks, they come into this White male–dominated environment doing those things that they do when they're back at home. And actually I guess assimilation is kind of a good word for it because that's really what you have to do. I have to understand ... and I've always understood that. I have to understand what it is in order for me to be successful in a White male–dominated world. I know that once I cross the line of my culture as a Black male and come into this culture I cannot be exactly that. I'm still me. But I know that I need to talk the way you expect me to talk in order to be successful. If I talk the way you expect a Black person to talk, I would get exactly what you believe a Black person deserves, which is nothing. That makes sense?

Our conversation then shifted to the topic of meritocracy and integration. I asked the participant to share his views on whether the Navy has achieved a meritocracy. When I defined meritocracy as being a situation where all decisions are made based on merit, he responded,

Maybe more so that way now. But it has not always been that way. And during my time I don't believe that to be correct ... that it was a meritocracy because I believe that if it's a meritocracy, a person can't say, "You won't make it." Well how can you say I won't make it, "You won't get advanced?" And the reason that person can say that is because ... if it is a true meritocracy, it would be strictly based on numbers, it would be based on performance. It would be based on those things. So that there's too much of a human element involved than there to be a meritocracy and the human element is, "You know what, I can change your write up to show that you are not my number one person." And if you're not anybody's number one person, you're not going to get advanced pretty much ... well, you could, but it's usually the number one people. I will make somebody else number one before I make you number one. And if you can use these forms of nepotism where I know somebody ... you know [for example] "My brother works over here and I'll make sure that your record is not the one that's, you know, first and foremost." So when that human factor's involved, the meritocracy doesn't work.... Ah, what I'm saying is that I think today, the military is closer to being a meritocracy that it was say 10 years ago. I don't think it will ever be ... a system that is based strictly on merit unless you find a way to strictly eliminate the human factor. If there are people involved, then, then it's a dynamic where anything can happen.

He continued by adding his views on the degree to which the military has achieved successful integration. He stated,

> How good are they at that? You know, the military, they are, they're pretty good at putting a lot of people together. They're not very good at helping people understand one another. Just because, because to me, when the military says "integrating," they're talking about "You've got all these people on the same ship together." Okay, now what? So now that you've got 'em all together, you know, that should not count as integration, just because you've achieved that. Okay, okay it's an integration, but what kind of education do these people have. You know, [for example] "I'm a White guy from Iowa, you know. Only White, only Black people or any other people of color I've seen is on TV. And here I am, I'm put in the same department as this Black guy from New York. We may wind up killing each other." So what is the Navy doing for understanding? I mean, really doing.

Chief Hines

Unlike many enlisted sailors, Chief Hines did not enter the Navy right after graduating from high school. Prior to enlisting, he had worked as an internal bank auditor. However, he left his employment at the bank to accept an auditor position at another bank but the position at the new bank did not materialize. He stated that he was unemployed for a while during the 1980s and he ended up enlisting in the Navy under those circumstances. When he enlisted, he planned on serving "maybe 4 years" and completing his degree prior to returning to civilian life. He had not given serious thought to how far he would progress within the Navy's rank structure because he did not fully understand what the potential was. He stated that no one had explained to him what it took to move to the next higher level.

I asked Chief Hines if there was a specific point in his career when he decided he would work toward becoming a Chief. He stated that he was motivated by the money and privileges that were associated with higher rank. Thus, he decided that for as long as he was in the organization, he wanted to go as high as possible. It was after he was selected for first-class petty officer that he decided that he wanted to become a Chief. He stated that he selected the route to Chief rather than an officer commissioning program because of the age requirements for the officer commissioning programs. The maximum age limit was 25 years old and he was ineligible.

When I asked him to discuss the process by which he advanced and to share any particular parts of the process that he found more difficult than others, he offered the following:

> The situation really is this, when I compared myself to most other African American males, I tended to be more ambitious than most of the others. I didn't have a whole lot of exceptions, except as affiliation, even though I had camaraderie with others who weren't African Americans. What I determined was that I could prove that I was just as capable as any non–African American. So I committed myself to a course of study that would propel me ... through my own diligence. I looked up every reference, I studied everything in the bibliographies and I went through every course. I reviewed over and over. As a matter of fact, on one of the particular exams, I aced it. I was driven internally for most of it. But what I found is that I had the perception that I was working harder than some of my peers who were not African American, in terms of the support that I received. Even when I made first class, I had a Chief who was not African American who seemed genuinely disappointed that I made first class.

I asked him to be more specific about the race of this Chief. He continued:

> He's White. He's White. I was the only individual in the command of one hundred plus people that made first class. The only one. He appeared genuinely disappointed that I made it because they had already caused my evaluations to reflect less than what I was accustomed to receiving.

As the conversation continued, I asked him if he considered this to be a barrier and if so, how did he deal with it. He replied,

> What it became for me [was] almost like a survivor's mentality. What it became for me is to find a way to outmaneuver the issues or measures. I'm not saying they were intentional. I think they may have been subconscious, but [I had] to outmaneuver those efforts to avoid becoming derailed in what I was as my goal. So to get back to what I talked about, that particular set of evaluations I alluded to, they were returned to Washington, D.C. because they were incomplete. That's the way they sent them out to Washington, D.C., incomplete. To the point, they returned them and said these need to be completed. Rather than the command taking the responsibility to retrieve the appropriate

information, they gave it to me and told me to do it. I simply retained those evaluations and never returned them. For me, to go out and do what they wanted me to do was for me to essentially be demoting myself. So I conveniently misplaced them, they never had a copy of it. So it came up as a missing evaluation, which was neither here nor there when I went to make Chief other than the fact [that] they wanted an accounting of why that wasn't there.

As our conversation about barriers continued, I asked him if there were any additional barriers or if those barriers changed or disappeared as he progressed up the chain of command. He discussed how he encountered the "good ol' boys' club" once he was selected for Chief:

Once I made it to Chief and considering all the off-duty education, I've done a lot of things. I also worked with some various platforms. I never received sailor of the quarter. I never received any of those accolades that others received... who were primarily White. Once I made Chief, I enjoyed [a] tremendous degree of latitude, for the most part. Then, once I arrived at a submarine training center, I encountered what is commonly known as the "good ol' boys' club." If I didn't gain the acceptance of the Master Chief and Senior Chiefs in key leadership positions, most of whom were White, it was pretty much a conclusion that I would not see Senior Chief. Essentially, that is exactly what happens. The irony is that most that did were those that were able to socialize with, those that catered to, this group of people, those that golfed with this group of people, those that drank with this group of people, [they] were those that received the more career enhancing opportunities. I didn't do that because it was very distasteful to feel like I was being somebody's groupie. I figured that my mind, skills, personal abilities, and my competencies were equal to, if not exceeding, theirs.

I asked him to define what is meant by the "good ol' boys' club" and he offered the following definition:

What the "good ol' boys' club" in my experience tends to be [is] the network of personal and social relationships that allowed people to receive opportunities, to receive information, allow people to connect to others that had the ability to assert some influence in decisions regarding their abilities to move. For instance, in this particular submarine command that I talked about, there was a female. They wanted the appearance of being supportive of women. This particular Chief, who was [in] her first year [as a] Chief, or what we refer to as a boot Chief, whose husband was the Master Chief who worked in an extremely high echelon command with an admiral. This individual that made Chief was ranked the number one Chief in the command her first year as a Chief. An exception was also made to allow her to go to one of the ships in the harbor to receive her surface warfare pin in 2 weeks. That's the kind of leverage that people received when they were connected to what I perceive as the "good ol' boys' club."

After listening to him discuss the barriers he perceived he faced, I asked him if there were times when he thought of quitting. He stated,

> There were. There's a point when the military went through an extreme financial shortage, the budget-cutting process. I was with the Marines then, and I could not understand — with everything that I had done, all my personal achievements, all my professional achievements — why I wasn't being promoted, which was not negating what others who had gotten promoted [had done] but it's questionable. People were left wondering "We know this person and know what they weren't doing." In an effort to overcome the fact that deployments, and training opportunities were very limited, I decided I would pursue my Master's Degree. One of the feedback statements I received was that "I get the impression that all you do is go to school." Here I am trying to present the fact that I'm still engaged in professional development, which does nothing but serve the purpose for what we're doing.... You have a better educated, better trained, and more knowledgeable individual. Rather than see that as an added value, it became a negative indicator that somehow I wasn't doing what I should be doing, even though the opportunity no longer existed because the money wasn't there to do those things. So taking the initiative to find an opportunity to distinguish oneself from their peers actually had a backlash.

I asked him if that caused him to consider quitting. He continued,

> It did, except for the fact that since I had begun down the road of my educational process, I was determined to stay for that reason. It was worth that at least. I still enjoyed a lot of the people also. I still enjoyed what I did. I guess what I really didn't like is what we refer to as the politics, the inequities that exist and the processes that allow us to get ahead and receive the opportunities.

Our conversation then shifted to when he first learned he was selected for Chief. This is often remembered as a highlight of a sailor's career. So it was with Chief Hines. I asked him to discuss his feelings when he first learned of his selection. He described his feelings:

> I remember, of course, when [it was] the time for the results to come to be disclosed. Everyone tends to be on pins and needles, just wanting to know "Did I make it?" I was on the Navy's hot air balloon team. I remember, we had gone to Pittsburgh. When I got off the plane, we had no idea the results had came out. I got out the plane and at the bottom of the ladder of this plane ... as we got off it — this was a commercial plane, so people could come out to the plane before you even started to de-board — this guy is like, "Is there a Chief ... up there. Is there a Chief ... up there?" Everybody turned around and said Chief...? I was like "Yes!! I made it!" Of course, by the time I got down to the bottom he was already haranguing me about being a Chief: "You call yourself a Chief? You're not a Chief yet!" It was a very happy day because I felt like I had overcome that hurdle on my own. I know that there were opportunities that presented themselves but I don't think it's luck. I truly believe it's opportunity and preparation. I had overcome this thing and I was just like most people and so happy.

After he finished recalling the good feelings of having been selected for Chief, I asked him if his prior experiences had caused him to have any negative feelings. His response was surprisingly positive:

> There really were no negative feelings that I carried over because I was in the mood that if I was going to do this, I would have to do the same things I've done when I've made rank every other time. The only thing that was totally out of my control was the board process, because I really had no influence on who they select. So I did everything in my control to make myself as selectable as possible. I didn't carry over any negativity.... No. Because all of that is true. What I felt was that even though I had to work harder, I still felt that I outbested the process. So for me, that was a personal victory. That, in itself, was worth celebrating and saying, "See, I knew I could do it." I wasn't going to carry anything else as a weight.

He stated that he did believe he made some significant accomplishments and that he made a difference while he was a Chief in the Navy. He explained some of his accomplishments:

> Absolutely, one of the first things I did as a Chief was in the field of equal opportunity. I had an opportunity to travel all over the Pacific theater. I traveled to Hawaii, to Washington State, down to California, all the way over to Singapore, to Korea, Japan, [and] Australia. All of these different places teaching and we would teach the curriculum but we also had opportunities to address reality that was going on in the lives of sailors. To be able to talk from one's own personal experiences, especially to a population that feels disaffected or disenfranchised, that feels like they were going through the same things that I know I felt like when I was trying to rise in the system. I felt I had an opportunity to inspire some people because some did actually say "How did you make Chief? How did you do it?" I had an opportunity to share how one had to wield themselves and have a focus on what they wanted to achieve and then simply believe it. Knowing that some things do lie outside of our control and just because you don't make it doesn't mean you don't deserve it.

I asked him to explain what he meant when he said, "Just because you don't make it, doesn't mean you don't deserve it." He explained,

> What I mean is I was privy to some backroom dealings later on in my career where a group of Master Chiefs got together and I was there. It was a very informal setting, private party more or less. I had been asked to go along to drive a particular Master Chief who knew me well. I've worked with him and he'd been having heart problems and didn't need to be driving. He asked me if I would mind driving him over there. So for that reason I was there. I recall them discussing individuals who they thought needed to be promoted, who they thought needed certain orders. They were determining people's lives and careers over their beer and barbeque chicken. These people had no idea. I know of an individual that actually had orders; his household goods had been

shipped; his family was prepared to go. They changed his orders right there and this guy was over in another country and had no idea what happened to him. I was thinking, that's going to be a real blow to him.

Returning to the accomplishments he said he made as a Chief, I asked Chief Hines if he was recognized for these accomplishments. He responded,

> Oftentimes the greatest rewards I received were from the students. They were very appreciative because it was the experiences, and the examples and instances that we could share of things we encountered with people that sometimes carried the greater impact of helping people to understand what goes on; how it needs to be dealt with or what some of the possibilities are in dealing with those things. More often than not, that was the greatest part that I enjoyed. Was I recognized for it? I received numerous letters of appreciation and letters of commendation here or there. I appreciated that, but I think I received recognition most everywhere I went from the people that would come up to me and say, "Yea I knew things like that happened and thanks for pointing that out to us so we know what to do in order to address it."

Chief Hines believes his work in the Navy will make a difference. In his view, making a difference in the life of even one sailor is an important accomplishment and one of which he is proud. As he described it,

> Systemically ... when you put it that way ... what comes to mind is systemically when you say long-term difference. The best analogy for me is the boy that was walking along the beach of starfishes where he picked up one and threw it out there. He picked up one and threw it out there and the father asked him, "Why did you do that? Don't you see all these others? That's not going to make a difference." The boy said, "It made a difference to that one." So here and there I made a difference to some and made that work.

While he stated that he believes he has made a difference, there are things that he wishes he had accomplished but did not. Among these, he states, is achieving the rank of Master Chief. He stated, "I wanted to make Master Chief because it would have given me the homage paid to Master Chiefs. It would have given me the opportunity to leverage that position and I had hoped for a higher position ... a command staff position somewhere where I can make a difference to try to enforce, to support those doing that EOA [equal opportunity advisor] job the same way I have."

I asked him, if he had the opportunity to start over again, would he do anything differently. He responded,

> Well, if I was starting over as a Chief, I can't say I would. I'll tell you why: because I did my best. I did things that were way beyond the scope of what I should have been able to do. Yet, I rose to the occasion and I performed. I would like to say yes, because there were opportunities that I wanted to take.

Earlier, I alluded to the fact that I had to find a way to get around the barriers that stood in my way. There were later opportunities that would have presented themselves that would have allowed me to still get to Senior Chief and quite possibly, ultimately Master Chief. By the time those opportunities came, I was a single father. At that point, I had the choice of pursuing my career to achieve my own personal goals, which I felt might be a little selfish when placed in the balance of being there for this child that was very much attached to me and, turning her loose to go chase something that was going to come to an end anyway. In terms of the career, in terms of opportunities, life for me has always been larger than the Navy. I wanted to have the greatest impact I could while there.

Our conversation then shifted to the topic of mentorship. This participant's experiences with mentorship were much different from many others with whom I have had similar conversations. In addition to not having experiences with formal mentorship, he stated that he cannot recall anyone whom he considered an informal mentor. Regarding formal mentors, he stated,

> Because of my unique position of being a squadron foreman, I did a lot of work independently. So I did not have much in the way of mentorships. Now I did see people here and there that I wanted to emulate. As far as being active mentors, I never really had any.

He added, "I can't say that there was anyone in particular that took me under their wing and said, "This is what you do." I pretty much had to learn almost everything on my own.

I asked Chief Hines if he was aware of the extent to which White sailors received mentorship. He was quick to answer:

> Absolutely. I was at a command in Guam. From the time I checked on, I saw there were people that were very much tied to the leaders of the command. There were other people that said "Those are the ones that are being groomed to take the positions to do this, that, or whatever." I would hear about the meetings before the meetings or the meetings after the meetings, the weekend cookouts that they had together or fishing trips, [or] golf outings. I never seemed to be able to penetrate that and of course the word was then that they, as I say now, that they conducted a lot of business during those periods of time. It had a great impact on those opportunities.

I asked him if he was ever invited to those outings and he stated that he was not. He added, "But I would also say there was also the perception on the part of others that I thought I was better than them because a lot of my time was expended going to school." He went on to describe those who were included in the group:

> I would say the majority was White. Even though I had a very close friendship with one of the other Chiefs who was always invited to go golfing with a certain Master Chief and his group of friends, I was still never invited. There was a certain Black Master Chief who seemed to distance himself, at least from me. I'm not quite sure what the purpose of that was. So he was there but I would attempt to talk to him but he just seemed to distance himself. So I just quit bothering because I felt like I was pursuing him and I didn't like that particular feeling.

I then shifted the topic of our conversation to more explicitly discuss race and the role it played in Chief Hines's career. When I asked if he believed race had made a difference in his advancement as he progressed through the ranks, he responded,

> Yes, I know it did because I've always been outspoken. What I mean is if I have an opportunity to address something, it didn't have to be contradictory, adversarial, or any of that. If I saw it, I was going to speak on it if I felt it needed to be addressed. I would get comments on my evaluations from my White superiors that would say as such: "tends to be a little outspoken." I'm not quite sure what that was supposed to mean other than the fact that "he speaks about things he should keep to himself." Of course the things I spoke about were true and everyone saw it and everyone knew it. I had an incident when I was on a particular ship. When they assigned berthing, it turns out they assigned all the minorities to a certain berthing area and all the Whites to a more desirable berthing area. This was in the medical department.

I asked him if he thought they deliberately assigned the berthing based on the race of those who must live there. He replied,

> I do. I do in that particular department because we have control over how we assign the people that come to our department. It's more than ironic that everyone that was a minority — everyone that is but Deb. By "Deb" I mean we had a bright young man that had an obvious drug addiction. He had been through non-judicial punishment several times. So he was put down there but everyone else — Hispanics, Blacks — that's where they were. Everyone White was placed up in this other more desirable berthing. This occurred over a period of time. Whether it was consciously done, I can't say, but the fact is that it happens and that's the way it was.

I asked Chief Hines if there were other examples where he believed race played a part. He provided the following response:

> Sometimes it's hard to say because there is no empirical evidence. I was in the training session in the department I was in and the officer told a joke in training. He said, "What did Abraham Lincoln say after the three-day drunk?"

I didn't know and a lot of the others didn't know. A Senior Chief in the back who hung a Confederate flag — and what the Confederate flag symbolized to me unequivocally at the time was someone that probably had racist tendencies — he stood up in the back and said, "I did what? I freed who?" ... The gentleman next to me, another Black male, just busted out laughing. I remember turning to him and saying "What the blank are you laughing about, man? The joke is about us being free."

He added that training opportunities were not affected by individuals' racial backgrounds. He also believed that there were times when race actually appeared to work in his favor. He explained,

Yes, because typically when I had the opportunity to speak. Rather, it was in training, I even had opportunities to do public speaking during special observances like Black history month or what have you. Professionally, as well as personally, race always helped me within the unit or various commands because when I spoke, I spoke intelligently. I was articulate and I knew how to convey a message. How race helped me was that I think it placed me above the expectations of some of the listeners who would not expect that from me because of my race. In a reverse kind of way, my race did help me because I performed above a level that I believe some expected for my race.

I then asked Chief Hines to discuss the extent to which he felt he was able to fit in and be accepted as equal to his peers. He responded,

As a majority, I don't feel I did, but it was situational. There were those random times where I did feel I fit in, where I was able to join the camaraderie, where they did seem to be those that did reach out and want to be inclusive. Those were random. There were times [when] I was not always ostracized or not included. There were those that were congratulatory in the things I had accomplished. It was just in the big picture [that] often times I was missing.

He continued by discussing the extent to which he believes his competence was accepted as equal to his peers:

Oftentimes I do believe that, because I worked independently a lot — I didn't have a peer group per se — but the overall quality of my work when compared and contrasted with those in other positions and other squadrons, I always did extremely well on inspections. Even when they created peer groups because they were necessary for advancement, I always had done more than the others and therefore that allowed me to stand out. So I think my competency was never really questioned. I always tend to have the respect for those that I have contact with. Those I didn't have contact [with] had no reservations about my abilities.

Continuing on the issue of race, I asked Chief Hines if he felt there was a need to change in order to fit within the predominantly White Navy organization. He responded,

> What I have learned a long time ago is that I have to be or possess the ability to be able to adapt to my environment whatever the environment is. I think it was Langston Hughes or Paul Lawrence Dunbar that talked about "We wear the mask." Sometimes I have felt like I had to put on a glass face and other times I was very genuine about the interactions I had in order to allow myself to be heard because there were many times I was speaking and I know that people were pretty much ignoring me. Even though what I had to say was relevant and pertinent to what was being discussed and was probably the solution that largely went ignored. So I developed methods for making myself be heard by attaching my comments to others who I knew was respected. I might attribute part of what I was saying to them in order to make it be heard and accepted.

Discussing other changes, he continued,

> I always maintained most of my cultural taste. I wore my hair the way I was going to wear my hair. I dressed the way I was going to dress. The only thing I changed was [I] continued to harness my speaking abilities. I expanded my vocabulary. Any changes I made were more intellectual than a physical outward change. I had no intention of stripping myself of how I perceived myself as an African American to be.

Regarding changes he made in his conversations, he acknowledged that there were times when he made changes to avoid offending White colleagues. However, there were times when he said he refused to change:

> There were other times when I simply wouldn't because I knew if I held my ground on a certain point or if I challenged certain thoughts or ideas that were being put out there, I knew it would make certain people uncomfortable. Sometimes I did. Sometimes I didn't. It just depended on where I was at the time.

As we moved to the topic of meritocracy, Chief Hines had some clear views on the claim that the Navy has created an organization where merit is the sole determinant of one's success. He shared those views with me:

> I totally disagree. I think that there are pockets and places where there are people that are conscientious and do strive for the meritocracy. I think that organizationally, that does not hold true. I've seen too many people receive opportunities, receive accolades, receive awards, receive rewards that they simply didn't deserve. I've seen people receive stuff just because it was somebody's turn so it might as well be this individual over here. I don't see meritocracy. I've sat on boards that were supposed to observe the merits of people, yet they were totally subversive in how they chose people for advancement, how to choose people for ranking, and to try to challenge it was almost like mutiny. [They would say] "This is the way we're going to do it. I know that's what that says, but this is my Chief's mess and this is how it's going to be." It was not based on merit. It was not based on merit.... Sometimes, I've seen

commands go out of their way to take someone who was an African American or Hispanic and was determined to make them the top-performing sailor, which denied others a fair opportunity and some of those others were White. So that's not what represents a meritocracy either.

I asked him if he could compare the state of the military's efforts toward creating a meritocracy to those of the civilian sector. He remarked,

> In all fairness, the meritocracy I'm not certain. The military is still overwhelmingly White male dominated. I believe it's going to continue to do so. I do believe that they have a greater awareness of the need to embrace the idea of striving towards meritocracy or striving toward an environment of inclusiveness that allows not only individuals but organizations to excel. To where the sum is greater than the individual parts. I do believe that's an ideal that they have. I just don't think they've mastered the methodology for making it a consistent reality for the majority of their sailors.

The conversation finally moved to the question of integration and the extent to which the military has had success in this area. I asked him to comment on the view that the military has had tremendous success with integration. He offered the following perspective:

> I would agree with that based on my experience. I have seen people that hold racist views and that's just where they are at that point in time. For me, I think [that] one of the best experiences of my military career is the exposure I've gained with different people, different cultural backgrounds, different ethnicities, socioeconomic backgrounds. Not only did I learn a lot, a lot of those other people learned a lot. I had an opportunity to break down stereotypes and I had an opportunity to have some of my stereotypes broken down. I think the military has provided an excellent opportunity in that regard for people to get in an up-and-close fashion to see the world through other people.

Master Chief Ivans

Master Chief Ivans enlisted in the military after hopes of playing collegiate football were dimmed by an injury in his senior year of high school. He had only received a partial scholarship to college, so he looked to the Navy as a means of learning a trade while also earning a salary. He was a teenage parent at the time and saw the Navy as a way of allowing him to take care of his responsibilities, learn a trade, and then return to college after a 3- or 4-year period in the Navy. He stated that he had never considered making the Navy a career until after his first 4-year tour. He ended up staying for an entire career and ascending to the rank of Master Chief.

Discussing the highest rank he thought he would achieve and whether he had considered the possibility of reaching the rank of Master Chief, he recalled,

> Ah, when I first joined the Navy I thought it would be successful if I could make E-6, because when I was in boot camp my two company commanders were E-6 [and] I thought that was a good attainment. So that was my focus. But once I made E-6 in the Navy, [and] ah understood more what Chiefs did, it was my hope to become a Chief. And, that's when I got the ambition that if I was to be a Chief I always wanted to be a Master Chief. And that's when I decided to make it a career and pursue that goal of becoming a Master Chief in the Navy. At the time when it came to be a goal and ambition of mine I really didn't know what it took to become a Master Chief. I focused on the next short term goal and readjust[ed] it to be my long term goal but I really didn't have the things, the steps in place because I had not met anyone that told me what I needed to do to prepare myself for promotion. It was pretty much ... I was on my own on my goals and what I decided to do.

After discussing the goals he had during the early years in his career, I asked Master Chief Ivans if he encountered any barriers as he moved up through the ranks toward Master Chief. He discussed what he perceived to be some unfair advantages provided to a White coworker:

> Well, I can tell you, one thing that I noticed in the Navy, ah, you can have the ability but ... you're not given the opportunity. I've always felt my abilities measured up with my counterparts. I considered myself a hard worker. And in my first 4 years in the Navy I went from E-1 to E-5. I remember that I consider my self working harder ... my other co-workers said I work harder but I didn't get the accolades the others got as a minority. And that's how I looked at it. Ah, I have no ... substantiated data that shows that, but I could say, for, for example me and another White male we came on onboard ship the exact same time within a week of one another. I completed my qualifications ... faster than he did, I would take on more responsibility but he would get the award, like he would be nominated for sailor of the quarter and I wouldn't. It was always some point that ... I could work on. And my first class, my LPO was a first class at the time, and my Chief were both White males and they would always tell me what I could be working on and I would do that, but I could see the things that he wasn't doing but he could still be recognized ahead of me. [A]lso in regard to school, when it came time for money for schools, ah, I would put in for a school, he wouldn't put in for the school and then he would be later on going to the school and I'd be told I have to wait [for the] next time. So I always thought that was an unfair advantage that I saw in my particular rating in communicating to other Black males that I knew on the ship in that particular expertise and ratings in other departments also.

In addition to discussing the scenario that he considered unjust, he discussed similar views that he said other Black males in his organization held:

It's common dialogue throughout my career with other African American, Black males that they feel that they work harder than, ah, the majority, particularly White males and they don't get the opportunities that some of them get, they're always told, "You can go next time" and next time don't seem to come and "This is what you need to work on." [T]here were other ratings in this department as well at sea and it was common knowledge with them that they would see the same things. Ah, the attitude with them was "no matter how hard you work, others [who] was not working as hard as you, particularly White males is gonna get the rewards, gonna [get] the awards ... get the ... schools ahead of you." So it was almost to the point where they felt as though you were being used. You were being used as a worker bee and not being rewarded. So it was somewhat de-motivating for them. And I took the approach that I was gonna make it motivate me. I was gonna consistently request the schools, ah, ask questions on what I could do better and use that as self-improvement and look at what I could do. And also continue [to] communicate what I was seeing as I felt unfairly because I always did bring that up to my LPO and my Chief, in particular that incident that was current with me, that I felt as though I was a harder worker than the individual that came onboard the ship the same time I did, same rating, same time in grade and it seem as though he got the awards and the rewards going to school before I did. I used it a motivating factor for me.

Master Chief Ivans stated that rather than allowing what he viewed as unjust treatment to serve as a de-motivator, he used it as a motivator. I asked him if there were any other ways that he dealt with the apparent unjust treatment. He added,

One thing I did that.... I actually, ah, raised my standards. Like whatever the Navy said was the minimum or as the standard, I would try to achieve it quicker. Because I said if I did the same as my peers I wouldn't be recognized. So I had to be, I had to achieve it sooner or faster and do a better job at it just to get equal recognition as they would get. So that was the somewhat motivating factor in how I dealt with issues as I continued to stay in the Navy.

I asked him if the obstacles about which he spoke remained constant or if they changed as he achieved higher rank. He said it did not change and then proceeded to discuss his experiences:

No, I can't really say it changed. I'd say a changing factor for me was when I became a first class and I was on shore duty, my first shore tour. I got my first mentor, the person that I considered a mentor and [who] took an interest in me and my career endeavors. The first person I can say that really had a big impact on me and the way that I looked at the Navy, it was a White Master Chief. Ah, at first, I took it as though he had an interest in ... my best interest because I was just learning about the military, but as time developed, this is my opinion of him, he would select certain minorities. He would, like, give you what I considered bennies for a selective period so it wouldn't bring any highlight on what his whole intentions were [which] was to hold other minorities back. So if you were new at a command, he would identify with some of your strengths and some of the abilities you had but when it came time for Sailor of the Year or when it came time to put someone in for an award, it went back to the same regime that I ... saw at sea. It was even going on on shore duty. Ah, it would come up "You're missing this [or you'd have] been my top sailor." Specific example: I was ranked [the] number one First Class but when it came time for Sailor of the Year, it was always mentioned what I could do more of. But then that's what I targeted on to say, awards are subjective. What I do is objective on my reports. And I always did a good job and ensured that it was documented so my reports were always objective. And it was always above par with my peer group so I was always ranked number one, but I never got any awards for some of the things I accomplished and I was never was recognized for Sailor of the Year or anything. And I noticed that with him, when it came time for that, he would only focus on my negatives. But at that same command when that particular Master Chief retired, a Senior Chief, a Black male, came onboard and he was able to mentor me and let me know some of the things that I needed to concentrate on if I wanted to make the Navy a career and if I wanted to pursue attaining khaki while I was in the Navy. So that's when my career turned around, when I was able to get that mentor.

He suggested that having the informal mentor was a turning point in his career. I asked him if, up to that point, he had ever considered giving up. He stated that he had:

I can tell you it was conflict and that was uncommon for me ... I could see that I was succeeding, but the stress of it and the dilemmas ... at what expense? Like to achieve, I was what you could call a rate-grabber. I made E-1 to E-8 my first time up, so but people would say what do I have to complain about, I'm making rate. But I, I could see where others [who] were making rate, wasn't doing what I was doing. Like, I did 3 straight tours at sea, which was uncommon for my expertise and the program that I was in. I qualified in Officer of the Deck underway. I was security manager, so forth. Items like that, that were far and beyond for my expertise ... and did get me promoted. But I knew if I didn't do these things, I saw others that were doing good jobs — ah, Black males — and not being promoted. So it was like, at ... the rewards were at what expense. And it was a constant dilemma with me to balance my personal life, my family and my, my Naval career. So I would look at it at times [and ask] is it worth it to what I'm trying to obtain. So it was always a period of "Hey, just let this go and go ahead and do something else."

However, he did stay and he proceeded to discuss why:

The reason I ultimately decided to stay was in talking with my family, with trying to be a role model for my sons, is that things are gonna be hard and so if I walk away from 'em, from something that I wanted to achieve, I felt as though I was giving in to the process that the Navy had at hand that only a select few Black males could achieve the status of Master Chief. So I took it as a personal motivator within myself that I was going to do everything I could that I knew of, and whenever they said, "This is what you're missing to obtain that," ah to present within myself to say I was a quitter. Even though at times I felt like the parallels were not even on what I was told I had to achieve in regard to merit than what I saw other counterparts doing, of my same pay grade, White males.

While he states that he had considered quitting, he did stay and recalls the feeling he had when he learned he had been selected for the rank of Chief:

Yes ... I can tell you. I can't speak for others but it's, it's one of the most vivid times in my life. Others like my first son being born and being married. When I made Chief I was at sea in San Diego. I had recently got aboard the ship, was a new crew member on the ship. Only probably 6 or 7 months, so I was still assimilating to the ship's organization. But my mentor had told me where I was, that I needed to go back to sea. So I did because I needed to pick up my warfare designator and, in my only opinion ... [that] was an item that I needed to make sure would not be something that would be singled out to say I didn't have. Others at that time were making Chief without it in my rating but, ah, I felt and from some of the advice from my mentor that I wouldn't be able to do that because I was a Black male. So I went back to sea to get my warfare designator and worked hard at it, achieved it in half the amount of time that it would take the average sailor to do it. The requirement is 12 months and I was able to do it in 7. And received a waiver from the CO to petition to take my board ahead of time so I could put that in my Chief's package. And when I got the report of it, it was like I was on cloud nine. It was like all the hard work had paid off and the things had fell into place ... on "if I do do this. If I went back to sea again and received this warfare designator then it would happen." And I was. I was selected.

He was clearly happy about having been selected for Chief in spite of the obstacles he said he had to overcome. I asked Master Chief Ivans if he retained any negative feelings about those barriers. He responded,

Yes, and I'd say it still lingers on today and like I said I talked to my mentor, [who] retired as a Senior Chief, an' I know he was definitely Master Chief material. He went on and he works at the port of San Diego as the VP of Human Resources admin., so forth, highly educated man. But he was able to pass on some things to me that I was able to use and I've tried to pass that on. But the negatives that I see, even in my day-to-day dealings with the politics in the Navy, I've sat on awards boards, I've sat in disciplinary review boards and saw how it's personality driven ... and with personalities, I feel race, gender and all that comes into play and most decisions are all made by White males. That, ah ... what's the word I'm looking for? How we equate the standards are totally different in that regard to ... especially on Black males. So that's been very difficult to deal with. I've been able to change some of that as a Master Chief. But ... one alone is not going to be able to make a dent into how the Navy has passed this along with tradition throughout the years.

While he believes the Navy has passed along these disparities over time, he does believe he made some significant accomplishments as a Chief, Senior Chief, and Master Chief. He discussed those:

> The biggest [success] I believe that I've made [is that] throughout my encounters I haven't let that make me become bitter. I've used it to become better ... a better leader, better father, better husband and so forth. And I've tried to instill that same standard in the others that I've mentored and met that even if you feel the standards are not parallel in regard to how you view on your accomplishment, don't become bitter because of it. Use that to become better. And, ah, looking toward achieving those standards to look for self-improvement and communicate with your chain-of-command when you feel issues are not on an even level, how it's measured at the command and how they administrate it in regards to discipline and in regards to rewards and recognition.... That you communicate with your chain of command; that you don't shut down. Because I think that's where I was sometimes in my career until I met the mentor that helped me. That others told me, "Just give up; shut down. And that's the way it's gonna be. Either you accept it or get out. So if you can't deal with it, get out." But I've tried to say, communicate to your chain of command, set standards, and use it as ... those standards to become better within that organization and not just withdraw and shut down.

I asked him if there was any accomplishment that he considers to have been his single most significant accomplishment. He shared the scenario that occurred when he was assigned to the minesweeper USS *Ingleside*:

> I can say when I was on a minesweeper, in *Ingleside*, when I came onboard the ship, it's very important for the Chiefs to work together. It appeared to me that the Chief's mess was somewhat divided. Only certain Chiefs could speak up, and so it went through the whole command like that. I was the first Black male Chief to come on that ship in some time. And it really set a tone for some of the Black male sailors that, that they ... I guess they had a role model to look up to. And it was somewhat disturbing in the Chiefs' mess at first because at first it was a challenge for them, on how they were gonna deal with me. I learned that by communicating within the mess, communicating with the XO and the captain, the views that I had, ah communicating the concerns [of] not only the Black sailors, but all sailors, and being listened to and seeing that implemented and have the Chiefs' mess rally and come together. I think that was a big accomplishment because it could have really definitely went in the other, opposite direction and the Chiefs' mess could have become divided more, but we pulled together and they started to ... because some of the White males, specifically the enginemen on that ship, I ... in my observation I considered them what I call a typical red-neck, each was on his own agendas all

the time and anybody who spoke something different than what he wanted to do was always against him and he was gonna try to get rid of him. So within my first 2 weeks on board, he tried to get rid of two Black males. And when we brought 'em in for disciplinary review board I pointed out to him that this was not uncommon. And what was he doing to mentor and to help develop him? And at first, me and him were really at odds but we came to develop a relationship, that I was not trying to tell him how to do his job. We were just trying to do business as a Chiefs' mess and other Chiefs seen that and they seen me standing up for what I thought was right, helping to pull the Chiefs' mess together and also pull that command closer together. So I think that's one of my top accomplishments.

Master Chief Ivans considered this to have been a major accomplishment. I asked him if he received any recognition for those things that he considered major accomplishments. He stated that he did not and proceeded to discuss another incident that he experienced on the ship where he was the only Black Chief or officer onboard:

> No, not anything other than what the other Chiefs got. But I was always told that I was the best Chief and my fitness reports, or what we call in the Navy, evaluations, showed that, ah, I was the number one Chief onboard. Rewards ... I have four less rewards than the other Master Chiefs would have but I've always been recognized for the things that I've done in my reports, my evaluation reports. And I will tell you this brings back a memory, on that ship ... it's not normal for me to be a damage control person in firefighting in the Navy but on that ship, it's a small ship, we all had to be gainfully employed. And I had to raise my knowledge of firefighting. So we're in a meeting talking about how we were gonna be paired up for the big inspection, and they were having problems with one of the leading firefighters on the ship and he was a Black male. And again, that same engineman said, "ah, we'll replace him." He was always thinking about "we'll fire a person." And we were looking at other way to do it. And so I recommended, pull him to the side and let him know how important he was to the team and to see how that would work. And the captain said he loved that idea. And he told me, "I'm glad we got you onboard because you're the H-N-I-C. And then everybody laughed and I didn't think it was funny. Okay so everybody laughed and I [don't] think they took it to mean anything. So after the meeting, I stayed back and I asked the captain what did that mean. And he laughed and he said, "Chief"—I was a Chief at the time—he said, "Chief, you've heard that before." And then I said, "No, captain, I'm not sure that I have. Ah, you used some acronyms. What does that mean." And then he told me that means, ah, "You're the head ... you're the head Black man in charge." And I said, "Sir, but that's not the initials that's H-N-I-C." And he said, "Chief, that's a compliment. Don't turn something and make it be something that it is not." I said, "But sir, that is offensive to me. If you thought that I said something that was in agreement with you, I would hope that you would not use that type of acronym in regards to me again." And he said, "Aw, loosen up, loosen up. We're all stressed

because we got a big inspection. The other Chiefs knew exactly what I was saying." And I said, "Like I said again, captain, I didn't consider it to be funny and I would not like to be referred [to] that way." And he said, "Point was taken."

As we continued our conversation, I asked him if he believed he had made any long-term difference in the Navy. He stated that he hoped that he has and he continued,

> I would hope that it has. But I can only say the impact that I have seen. I go to retirement ceremonies and the individuals that, that worked with me that retired before me, and they thank me and they say I made a difference. So that's all that I can take from it. And I can see, I see more, ah, Black males in khakis than when I came through the ranks. So I would have to say that maybe things have changed in regards to that. I haven't looked at any numbers just specifically in regards to ... because the Navy is changing. More ratings are merging together so I'm not able to see ... because I was a radioman. They merged with the DP, Data Processors, and we became Information Technology Specialists. To see how the numbers rank up and so forth with that because the Navy has changed. A lot of ratings have merged together. I can share another story. I recently went to a retirement ceremony up in Jacksonville for a person that I made ... acquainted as a friend. [This] particular Master Chief, she completed 30 years of service — Black female — and she was thanking, she was saying how she thought ... thanked me for some of the guidance I shared with her through our encounters as our paths crossed and so forth. And the caterer was there. And I noticed it but I just hadn't put my finger on it, how many Master ... Black Master Chiefs that were there. And then the caterer was setting up and she said, "I wonder if this is for real." She said, "I've been catering a lot of events and — West Coast and East Coast — and I've never seen this many Black Master Chiefs." So then that made me take time and I looked around and I said, "You know something, I've never seen this many black Master Chiefs together in one place either." So then I said, "Maybe things are being looked at and things are changing." Because that was not common at all when I came in the Navy in '86.

While he acknowledged seeing positive changes, when I asked him if there were any things he wishes he had accomplished but did not, he again focused on improving promotion opportunities for sailors:

> [Long silence] I'm trying to think because that's a really good question. I, I wish that maybe that I could have had more impact. I sit selection boards ... and it was recently. And I wish I could have made Master Chief sooner and I think I could have had more impact[ed] on individuals making Chief. Because I understand the process now. I wish I ... knew ... understood the process sooner and I could have shared more and I think I could've impact more sailors' career paths ... on what they needed and what they were missing that were rightfully deserving on putting on khaki. Because I've seen some good

sailors retire as first class. And I've seen some really good sailors retire as Chief that I know was Master Chief material.

If given the opportunity to start over again as a Chief, he said he would start pursuing higher education sooner. He also stated that he would work to improve the training provided to sailors and work on improving communications in the Navy.

I then directed our conversation to the topic of mentorship. He had mentioned earlier about the impact informal mentors had on his career. I asked him if he had any experience with formal mentors. He responded:

> As I understand the question, formal mentor would be that the command directed it and the command identified with it. It was not formal. It was a relationship that the individual seek me ... that he saw potential in me and then from that point, I took him as an example and treasured the advice and the guidance that he shared with me and I made it formal that he was my mentor. And I guess that would be in an informal capacity in regard to how the military looks at it.

He spoke positively about the quality of the informal mentorship he received, stating that this mentor looked out for his best interest:

> Well I can really only say as I look at it from today, I mentioned the first White Master Chief, I can say that at the time I thought he was a mentor. I come to understood he really wasn't. So I can only say I really had one person that I ever, I can call an informal mentor. And that person told me the potential they saw in me, my abilities ... skills and abilities, gave me books to read on how to develop the weaknesses that he identified in me. He challenged me on the hard stuff when he felt as though my ... the conduct or the example I was setting was not to the standard that he thought it should be for me. Ah, from the day he retired, he kept in contact with me and always asked what was my next endeavor, what was my next goal, how I was looking at attaining it, and what he could do to help me do that ... to achieve it. He would put me in contact with other individuals that, ah, in the military that could help me in that endeavor ... that have been down that road. So I just felt he took my best interest at hand from professionally to personally. So he really helped me to prosper.

He then offered an interesting comparison of the mentorship White sailors received, compared to that received by Black sailors:

> My point was that up until I became E-6 and I met the mentor that I still call my mentor today, I had never had a mentor. A White sailor gets a mentor, from my observation, the day he walks on board ship or the day they get to their first command in the Navy. And they're passed on [to] each command. It's ... they're called ahead and set up with somebody else to take that person on from that command. It's like ... it's always been a formal ... informal mentor program for White males ... and even White females are taken care of the

same. If you're a Black male, it's just by the luck of the draw that you'll find someone who will take you ... ah, take interest in you and your career endeavor. Because a lot of the Black males in the Navy that I have encountered, they never had a mentor so they never knew the importance of it. But that's changing in the Navy today. But when I came in in the '80s, it was more like "That's how it is. Just get over it. That's how it's gonna be." They just ... the extras, ah, White males gonna get taken care of. You're gonna wait and see what's left over. And but no one understood that it was because of the mentorship. And I can even see ... I know the difference in how Filipinos communicated with one another on my first ship. It was like, the term used "the Filipino connection." Because they someone had that same mentorship going with sailors when they came aboard the ship that I didn't see with the Black sailors.

I asked him to discuss the role he believes race has played in his career. He clearly believed race has played a role in his career:

Ah, like I said, I can't look at the numbers, but from my observations and what I know I experienced I think it definitely did. Race was used in two ways with me. I met other sailors that worked hard — Black males — that were good at what they did [and] didn't get the recognition they deserved. At the same time I didn't, but I didn't let it stop me and say it wasn't, that it was unfair and that I wouldn't keep trying. And like I explained, I seek that knowledge wherever I had to get it from. But it shouldn't be that way but it can make you, as a Black male, say "No matter what I do I'm not gonna succeed. There's only so much I'm gonna get." And I feel as though in the Navy, the numbers are counted [as] "how many Black males I'm gonna [let] come through this door. Okay, I got three right now. No matter how good you are, you're just one day too late. So you're gonna wait because I can only let so many through right now." So it's not only the Black male's ability. It's somewhat on timing and it's somewhat on the organizations that individuals get at. And it shouldn't be that way because any White male can go and achieve if they do the right thing. But any Black male can't go to organization and achieve. It comes back to the word I've always heard: "timing." Whatever that ... whatever that means.

He continued by providing a specific example of the impact race had on his career:

Yes. Ah, I finished my qualifications to be import duty radioman. Okay, the same White sailor, we came on the ship. He said he didn't wanna do the qualifications because it meant more work. So he would rather just stay in another section and work for somebody. So I said if I finish my qualifications, I would have my own section, and I wouldn't have to work for someone on duty days. I completed the qualifications and I was a Seaman at the time. A Second Class was transferring so we were gonna need another duty radioman in the section ... the radioman was gonna be going ... the ship was in five sections. We would be going in four. So we definitely had a job available. I finished the qualifications; passed my board. Then this Senior Chief, was a White male, turned around and said, ah ... this is the point of the story that helps to bring it home. Me and him came in the Navy at the same time within one week of one another. He had the opportunity the same as I did — but I wasn't planning on staying in — to be accelerated advanced to Petty Officer Third Class. I decided not to take it because I was not gonna stay in the Navy. We did the same thing. Once he got to the ship and I was doing better than him and so forth and I was gonna be the next duty radioman, the Senior Chief went down — at first talked to him — went down to personnel, they backdated all his records and said that he wanted to be a Petty Officer. They gave him back pay, made him a Petty Officer and then put him in the section with me, for me to work for him when he wasn't even qualified for the job. So he was the Petty Officer. I was qualified and I worked for him. So I knew definitely race played into that. He didn't want me to be a Black seaman as the duty radioman. So, ah, he was alright in looking at that for the White male to be unqualified and do the job instead of for the Black male to be qualified and do the job. So I believed race definitely played an issue in that.

Master Chief Ivans did not believe that race was always a negative factor in his career. He stated that there were times when race was a positive factor and he discussed one of those times:

Oh yes, without a doubt. Ah, I can share that when I became a Senior Chief and I became an Equal Opportunity Advisor, working with a captain and we was getting ready to make a brief and I was ... some of the comments that were said, and he said, "I wouldn't brief that ... I wouldn't have allowed that to be briefed — but that was good for the admiral to hear that — if you weren't Black." So "If you weren't a Black male and understood that, then I [would] have allowed that." So it was a good thing because of race there because it was very valid points that were coming out of this organization that needed to be heard at the flag level. Definite changes came about. But what he actually told me was that if it was a White male in that job he wouldn't have let that been brought to the admiral. So nothing wouldn't have happened for the command.

Master Chief Ivans seemed to see race as a factor in many different areas in his career. Even when discussing the topic of training, he believed race was a factor:

Yes, I can tell ... from my second ship. I'm not mechanically inclined, but in my job we do communications and systems. I consider myself highly comfortable, competent and capable, ah, technical in regard to equip ... communication equipment. So I wanted to go to be expert satellite operator, one of the top schools for my rating. We had got money for it. I was in line for it. We also needed a teletype repairman so I was always the top communicator, ah, was doing the job without the training. The training would definitely help me promote. We got the money for the school. I always thought I was going, was never told otherwise. When it came time for the school date, they sent a White male and I didn't know anything right up to ... I always thought I was going. I requested the school numerous times, I was doing the job without the training, and then what was finally told to me when I put in a request to ask why I couldn't go was that I was doing a fine job without the training. They wanted to train somebody else up to be able to work with me. So that person actually never really did the job. When they came back, they transferred and got a bonus because of the sch ... what we call in the Navy NECs. They show that you're qualified to do the specialty. But I remained doing the job and this person got paid the bonus and never did the job and went on to another command.

While he seems to see race as impacting many different areas of his career, he does believe that he has been able to fit in and be accepted as equal to his peers. He stated "I've been able to communicate across race lines and the gender lines. So I consider, I've been accepted ah, reasonably easy in the open, in the workplace." However, he also states that, outside of work, he is not invited to as many social events as other Chiefs and Master Chiefs are.

In addition to feeling that he was generally accepted as equal to his peers, he also stated that he believed his competence was accepted as equal. Further, he stated that he was often viewed as being an exception to other Blacks, a sentiment that he rejected. He discussed this:

This is what I've always been ... always felt and been told sometimes. "Ah, others, Blacks complain about they want the assignments or want the job but they don't do a good job. You will take on responsibilities and you bring excellent results." So I ... that's the only thing that I've had a problem with. At times, individuals try to use me to say "you're the exception." I'm not the exception. I've met people that were far sharper than me; that were more educated than me; ah, and it was even as hard a worker as I am. But how they communicated that to the chain of command was different [from] how I communicated to the chain of command. So I'm not the exception. I can say I'm blessed that, ah, I got the right organizations at the right time and I'm able to seek out people that will support me in the goals that I had. Even if it's not my immediate supervisor, I've been able to find people in the organization that will stand up for me . I've been told ... I've not seen eye-to-eye with my supervisor at times. But others in the organization — may have been the Chief Staff Officer or the XO — but [they'd] always see the hard work that I was doing and would not let the person out to get in the way of me rightfully getting the type of report or evaluation that I should get.

As we continued discussing his competence, he offered a blunt assessment of whether his competence was accepted as equal to his peers who were White men:

No. It ... I couldn't say that. I've been accepted by my competence as what I bring to the organization. I don't really even believe it's graded on the same scale because they ... other White males don't try to see if a White male is competent in what they do. And then ... let me try to communicate ... as a White male you can be incompetent and still be a supervisor in the Navy. But as a Black male, you ... it would be documented and you would be removed for incompetence. So I don't know if I'm answering that question but that's, that's how I view it.... Not even graded on the same scale. In fact, if you're a White male — and I've worked for many — they'll tell you "I don't have a clue," but still get good reports and advance as high, up to par ... and they'll take credit for your work. But [if] a Black male was to make that comment, they wouldn't last their tour of duty. And it's always challenged — your competence — because any little chance that someone can say that you may lack a little knowledge in an area, it's gonna be monitored closely to see if it's a, a glitch in your armor that can be penetrated. That's just my take on it.

Master Chief Ivans then offered a thoughtful discussion addressing the question of whether he believes he has changed for the purpose of fitting in. He stated, "I've really gotten to know myself on how I react to certain things. Ah, I address issues a solution-oriented way instead of identifying problems and I feel a lot of Black males, they bring problems and say 'this is what's wrong.'" In his view, he addresses issues in a different way than many Blacks do. Then he added:

I've really seen situations where, actually I call it scripts were written to get certain Black males to react in a certain way so that they can be labeled in the organization. And I don't know if I've said that in the interview. If you show up as a Black male, within days or weeks, a label is put on you on how White males, and then how the command, will perceive you. And that label stays on you until you react and you justify or until some other White male helps you to remove that label, if it's unfavorable.

When I asked him about his ability to fit in with his White colleagues, Master Chief Ivans quickly responded:

No, because I haven't tried to be accepted in a social function with White males. At work, I've always made sure that if it's not offensive and it's within policy and standards and procedures of that organization, then individuals be able to be who they are and I'm able to be who I am. Ah, I can tell you, like dress codes for leaving ... the ship. I've seen that be in question because sometimes it seems like it's targeting a specific race. Ah, but I think, in my opinion I think that's more of a social gathering and I've never been big on that. I've never been a big social gatherer. I was married young. I came in the Navy. I was married at 18. Most of my time in the evening was spent at home. But I can see how that can come into play with individuals more frequently on the base, like the base club and stuff like that. I can see where that could've been an issue.

We ended our conversation with a discussion of the extent to which the Navy has created a meritocracy and a success story with integration. He was emphatic in his response to my query about whether the military has created a meritocracy:

> I would totally disagree. It would be hard for the military as a whole to ever do that because the military ... its structure is based on certain races being certain ranks at certain places. So if it's based on merit it may not present the ethnicity across the board that it would want. And also if it's based on merit so many Black males would still not be in leadership positions as ... how I look at is, White males, right now White males make predominately the selections for enlisted promotions. I'm not sure in regards to ... I know it's more White males totally across the board and officer's ranks the same but I'm not sure how their promotion boards work. But I know the board I sat, more than merit came into play in the discussions I heard.

He even suggested that awards were not distributed based on merit. When asked about them, he was quick to say, "No. Predominately those things are done based on personality. From, ah ... who you comfortable with and who you know. The particular things that were just asked of me I think are done less on merit than merit."

Similarly, he stated that he believes the military has had only limited success with integration. As we wound up our conversation, he explained his views on the Navy's success with integration:

> I would say the military has integrated on a tolerance to meet the mission but has not done anything in regard to make anything better, ah, create better race relations. It's all mission-driven ... what we need to put emphasis on for this time period to get us through this particular mission or this particular conflict, rather. And then positive initiatives are put on race relations at that time.

Master Chief James

Master Chief James is a native of Richmond, Virginia. He enlisted in the Navy in 1984 after being encouraged to do so by his cousin of the same age. Referring to his cousin, he said, "He came to me and told me that the military was a way for us to go in, get a education, learn a trade, then actually we could go ahead and get BMWs." His cousin told him that the military background would make it easier for them to get the credit references to purchase their new cars. Additionally, he said he was not a "college-minded individual" and that he did not want to put his mother through having to finance his college education. Thus, enlisting in the Navy appeared to be an opportunity to get some of the things he wanted out of life without burdening his mother. When he took the ASVAB — the military entrance examination — he scored high enough to select almost any Navy program of his choice. The recruiter discussed the advanced electronics programs in submarines and he entered that program.

Like many others who enlist, he had not planned on staying in the Navy for an entire career. However, his first enlistment was for a 6-year period and much of that time was spent attending military schools in Virginia Beach, near his home town. He stated, "Well by the time ... the first 3 years went by quickly. The next thing I know, I was in ... on a boat. The Navy told me, hey, I can go ahead and go back to VA Beach again you know for 9 months and then follow on school to go to the tender in Kings Bay, Georgia, for 2 years. So what happened, it kinda built on itself. I was having a good time." He ended up staying for an entire career and being promoted to Master Chief.

I asked this participant if he had given any thought to how far he might progress while in the Navy and he responded,

> Well, I would take the rating exam every 6 months, okay, and sometimes I would study, sometimes I wouldn't, you know. Because I had it in my mind that they weren't gonna advance anyone anyway. They may make four or five guys out of maybe the three or four hundred that were taking it. So I kinda had made myself believe that the reason I wasn't advancing was because the tests were set up for me not to advance. Well when they did everything back and said, "Hey, the day you guys need to decide, what you gonna do." I sat down and said [to myself,] "Okay, said Okay, look, I've been in the Navy for 9 years. I'm a Second Class, E-5. At the time we only had maybe four of us. Four of my ... ah ... guys that I work with that were E-6s anyway. If I wanted to advance in this Navy, I had to get somewhere where I didn't party, I didn't go out and socialize, I'd sit there and focus my attention on advancing, on my job, on my rate, and finding out and knowing everything I could about my job. Well I knew if I went to Kings Bay, Georgia, we're basically moving the party from Virginia Beach to Jacksonville, FL. At the time, I knew one person out at Bangor, Washington. So I decided, you know what, that's where I needed to go because usually, that guy would be out at sea, again, I have no one really to socialize with, I've gotta be focused on my job. So if I'm gonna stay in this, you know, this man's Navy, I need to go out there. I need to focus on advancing. And, ah, I got out there in '93, I went to school, I went to the boat, my first ship ... my first submarine out there in '94. I got there as a second-class petty officer and I left there in September of '98 as a Chief.

He stated that once he settled down and focused on promotions, he moved up the rank structure. In doing so, he did not believe there were any steps that were more difficult than others. When asked, he responded,

> Not really. The way, I mean the way the system is set up it was ... all the information was really there and it was available to everyone. It depended on the mindset that you had on acquiring that information and putting it to use, you know. And I really, I really blame it on myself from the fact that I made myself believe that it wasn't available, you know. But it was. And then when I sit back and I look at it and I think about it. That information, all that information was there. I was, I was caught up in the, in the party, you know. We were all partying; we were having a good time. Everyone around me, all my, ah ... all my friends were E-5s also. So I didn't feel like I was losing anything or missing out on anything. Every once and awhile one of 'em would advance off of the test. But still the number of those that weren't advancing was greater. So I didn't feel that pressure. I didn't feel like they were leaving me.

Having previously indicated that barriers existed for him due to the decisions he made, I asked Master Chief James if he experienced any obstacles other than the ones he had placed for himself. For him, the absence of African American role models was viewed as a barrier. He discussed this issue:

> I think one of the biggest things [about] being on a submarine was the fact that there weren't a lot of African Americans there. So there weren't a lot of people that I could go to and relate to. I, I didn't see any Black Master Chiefs, you know. I didn't see any Black Senior Chiefs. I think I may have seen ... I saw, I remember seeing one Black Chief and it seemed that he had an attitude. You know, like he was above. 'Cause I remember guys wouldn't really socialize with him because he kinda ... talked down to 'em. You know, so they felt that ... I didn't see somebody to model myself after. You know, ah, at the time, [in] my rate, the senior person onboard may have been an E-6.... There really wasn't a whole lot of E-7 MT Chiefs, because usually what that person would do when they made E-7, they'd cross over to fire control. You know, so I remember being onboard ... my first submarine I was onboard, there were two ... there were three Black people on board. With the submarines, you have two crews, of approximately 180 personnel. Okay, in the MT Division there's approximately 19 or 20 people. Out of the, say, 40 personnel, there were three of us that were Black ... alright, one other guy on my crew and one other guy on the other crew. Ah, yea, my first underway period, I think there may have been 10 Blacks total out of the 180 people on the submarine. Ah, my next command I went to, sea-going, was a tender, which had more Blacks as a whole on the entire tender. But again, still in my, my rate there probably were, I think the most were four of us at one time. That was four out of maybe 57 guys, there were four Blacks. Later on when I went back to a submarine, there were ... for 4 years, I was the only African American on my crew. On the other crew, there was one other African American. So we were the only two again out of 40 individuals.

He focused his entire response on the limited number of Blacks in the command and in his particular rating. I asked him how this impacted him and he responded,

I'm not gonna say that it didn't motivate me, because at the time I had to go with, I guess personal goals, personal accomplishments, you know. Hey, I just wanted to exceed, excel. I just wanna go ahead and do all the things I could do at the time. I remember having, ah, I remember having a Command Master Chief at the time that I would have sworn at the time that ... his name was even Tex. You know, I would have sworn that this guy, you know, was racist. And because this guy, this individual, when he talked to me, we never made eye contact. You know, he was carrying on a conversation and looked almost all around and at everything but me. And I remember I made Chief with him ... and I told him, I said, "You know, eh isn't it just a funny world that you and I now belong to this same fraternal order, you know." And this guy ... with his tobacco in his mouth, ... [said], "Yea, who would've ever thought," you know.... That was, that was, I was doing something that, you know, no one else [who was Black] was doing at the time. [I]t did make it harder because I didn't have that role model. I didn't have that guy that I could go to and have him explain to me how it felt to be in the Chief's quarters ... and be an African American. You know, what do you do ... is it different? I didn't have anybody like that. I was blessed, I was truly blessed in that I did have some senior Caucasian individuals that looked out for me. And sometimes even when I didn't know they were looking out for me. You know, I had a Senior Chief who was like "Hey ... you need to go qualify, you know, Chief of the watch." And I'm like, "Well, hold up. You've got this guy, this guy and this guy. Why aren't you making them?" They're like, "Hey, you need to do it." And because that guy made me do some of the things I did, I didn't know it at the time, but he was setting me up for the next highest pay grade and I remember that. I use that now when I talk to my guys. [I say] "You may not believe it at the time and you may believe this guy is messing you over. You know, but sometimes when people make you do something, maybe they see something in you that you don't see in yourself or you don't recognize."

I asked him if things changed for him as he moved up the chain of command. He responded,

I think as I moved up, let's see, when I made Chief, I left the submarines and went to recruit division commander at Great Lakes and became an RDC. Being there was a big eye-opener because of the say 650 RDCs there, there was only three of us that were submarines, or submariners. Okay, because of that, I go to see first hand what the surface community was like ... how those individuals dealt with situations. And it was totally different from the way we on the submarines did, you know. Submarines, we tend to think ... at the time we thought that we were a big part of the military but in actuality, we're only 7 or 8% of the entire Navy. Ah, watching and dealing with these individuals—and these individuals had more Black, ah African American, Chiefs. There was a few African American Senior Chiefs, you know. Mind you I also saw then where there was, I say, an African American Senior Chief. And this individual felt like he was above everyone else. And I didn't know whether that was because of the surface structure, the way they brought 'em up where you felt that you were, you know, higher than anyone else. But I saw that in his demeanor. You know, I remember one time I had to go talk to him about something. Someone pulled me to the side before I went there and was like, "Hey, I know we're told, you know, taught as Chiefs that we're all equal and you can say whatever you want to each other." But they were like, "Just remember though, he's a Senior Chief. And he's gonna want that respect as a Senior Chief. "And I couldn't understand that. That was something totally different from anything I'd ever dealt with before. You know, and then later that individual made Master Chief [and] he still had that same demeanor about him, you know, like he was somewhat god-like. So that was ... I've always learned that you learned something from everyone and I learned then that I would never be that way. I would never be unapproachable by anyone. You know, so because of that ... I ran into circumstances that I would see junior personnel and they'd be like.... "What do I got to do to be like you?" And I'd say, "First of all, you have to remember that you can be and you can do whatever you wanna do." You know, the only limits that you actually have are the limits that you put on yourself. But you sit there and listen to society or listen sometimes ... even to that friend, you will for some reason believe that you can't do something or that you're hindered from doing something, and it may not be true. You may tend to be your own hindrance. The system has a lot of things out there available to you. For a lot, for some reasons, we, as African Americans, may not grab it as quickly as that Caucasian. Maybe it's because we don't have it instilled in us that you're what it's there for. You should go for it. It's there for you like it is for everybody else. And maybe that comes from the fact that we don't see a lot of African Americans in the senior leadership positions. So you feel because you don't see 'em there, then maybe that's not for me. Maybe it's not meant for me to be there. But you've gotta think around that, you know. My big thing [is] to be an example to everyone. You know what, I'm a average guy. You know, I ... a lot of time ... I do as much as I've gotta do to get everything done. And there are times I won't go that extra step, that extra block, you know. So in the blessing that I've had to get to where I'm at, I make sure those guys know that, "You know what, as long as you continue to strive to go forward, you know, you can. And the first time you stop or the first time you go backwards, it's up to you to get yourself going. It's up to you to keep moving up."

Master Chief James was very positive about the opportunities for junior sailors and their ability to achieve. I asked him if there were any times when he had considered quitting. He stated that he had never considered quitting. Additionally, he stated:

Later, as a Chief, when I was in Great Lakes, I got married. Then I had a wife and daughter, so that definitely took that "quit" out of my vocabulary. So now I strive to be an example and role model for them. When I got to Great Lakes, then I had 90 recruits that I had to be the example for.... Well, since making E-9, I've now got 8 years left to be in this Navy if I choose to. Well, this year I'm putting in a Warrant Officer package, okay. That way I have another opportunity to go to another area of the Navy and advance to show progression and again to be an example to, let's just say, ah, African American sailors, but to any sailor that I can say he can do it also, you know. I see sailors ... I was in the commissary one day and a sailor walked by and came back to the aisle I was in and came down and shook my hand and he said, "you know what, Master Chief? I've been in the Navy for 7 years and you're only the second Black Master Chief I've ever seen." You know, I've been here in port and I've seen sailors that have come and told me, "You know what, I'm glad to see you, because I've never seen a Black Master Chief ... not submarines. I've seen a couple on the surface [side], but I haven't seen 'em in the submarines." You know and that makes me feel good. I travel ... my command doesn't understand why I won't sit in the office. They don't understand why whenever something's going on, say, in Jacksonville, or something in Norfolk, or something in D.C., or even in Bangor, Washington, I'm saying, "Hey, let me go." You know, I have to go. I have to go so that other sailors can see that, hey, that they can do it too. And there is something out there. That there's somebody out there that's doing these same things that everybody else is doing, you know. And like I said, if he can do it ... he makes mistakes. He laughs at jokes. If he can do it, I can do it too.

I then moved our conversation to the time Master Chief James made Chief and how it felt when he first learned he was selected. As with many Chiefs, this was a pleasant memory for him. He shared how it happened and how he felt:

Ah, I remember because I had duty that Friday night and [for] some reason, the results came out that Saturday. I'd only taken the test one time, so it's my first time up for Chief ... eligible for Chief and ah, I remember I was in my apartment in Washington State and this guy calls me: "Is this.... " [I say] "Yes." [Then he goes] "Is this ... ah, you know, such and such and such? And such." I'm like, "Yes." "Well hey, congratulations." And I'm like, you know, "What are you talking about?" "You're on the list for Chief." And I remember sitting there and I'm thinking, "It can't be." I was the guy who, ah ... you want me to tell you all the ... all the wickets you gotta make to make Chief? I mean you had to be the EP [early promote] ... you had to did this; you have to have done this; you had to have done this. There were at least three things they told you you had to have done to make Chief that I hadn't done. So when my name came up, I was like "My goodness! Are you playing with me?" ... And then it was confirmed because now I was being put in the position where, let's say, I was that Chief. And everything that I'd ever been told about the Chief was that Chief was all that and a bag o' chips. So I, I actually began to question myself and, even then I had no other Chiefs at my command that were African American that made it also. So now you've got a command that's predominantly Caucasian that just made two African American Chiefs. And that was it. So you could tell they were trying, you know, it was different for them also because now they had to, you know, learn us, figure us out. There was no other African American in the quarters, or in the mess. So now they had to accept us into that, their brotherhood. And, you know, they brought us in with open arms. With open arms, they brought us in, and they schooled me; they taught me; they talked to me. They educated me on everything they felt I needed to know. But since then, like I said, making Senior Chief, and then having to bring other African Americans …. ah, I felt sometimes like I had to keep my guys motivated, especially the African Americans.

As he continued to discuss his experiences making Chief and how he felt, he brought up the issue of affirmative action and the misinformed views that he had and which were held by some of his White colleagues:

I used to believe … I was one of those that believed, when I first made it, you know what, they had to make me because I was African American and they gotta make a quota. They've gotta make so many of us, you know. They gotta make so many Hispanics. They gotta make so many, you know of this. I believed that up until I sat the board myself this time. And when I sat the board, not once did anyone ask what anyone's race was while we were making our decisions as to who was qualified or who should be selected. When, of course, I'm sure when they broke up the demographics on the computer, that had all that on there … but not once did we consider that when we were making the selections ourselves.

So that was a good thing. That sorta made me feel, "You know what, I did truly make it off of my merit alone and it's the thing that did it and it had nothing to do with the fact that I'm African American and the fact that they had a quota." And unless they change it this board, like I said, I saw no pictures and I saw nothing in it that said they were trying to meet a quota when we made our selection. You know what though, the thing with that, the sad thing with that though, it's not so much, I really didn't see so much with the African Americans, but I saw it more with my Caucasian counterparts. You can tell sometimes … you can hear it behind our back or whatever. "Oh they made him … they had to make him, you know, because you know they had to make so many…." They were using it as, like, a reason why I was being selected each time I went up, you know. A lot of these guys — because I went from West Coast to East Coast — a lot of 'em had no idea who I was anyway. They couldn't even tell you who I was, you know. But they figure when they saw that I was African American, "Oh well, they had to make him." You know, they knew, they know Jim Bob or Billy Bob who had been in this program for so long, you know. [So they would feel that] he's the one. They should make him because he's been the squadron guy or he's been this. They have no idea what my career path has been like … the jobs I've taken on or how I had did while in those jobs. They just took for granted that because I'm African American, the reason I made it is because they had to make so many. And I do believe that because I've heard it from someone that they told it to who may have confided in me and believe that's what they did. So it was interesting on that side.

He expressed some strong feelings about the perceptions that some of his colleagues had of him and how they believed affirmative action affected his career progression. Further, he suggested that those White sailors believed that affirmative action equates to quotas. I asked him if, given his experiences, he had any lingering negative feelings that followed him into his role as Chief, Senior Chief, and Master Chief. He responded,

> Well, not ... I didn't. I think if anything, looking back, I knew that, you know, I was almost a 16-year second class. And I look back and I'm thinking, "Gosh, if I had went ahead and did that same focusing that I did that last year, 5 years, I could have been trying to be the next Force Master Chief or MCPON [Master Chief Petty Officer of the Navy.]" But it took me a while to get to that level within myself, you know. I think I was more upset with myself than the system or anyone else because, like I said, the opportunity was there. All those same books that everyone else read, anything, any billet that anyone else went to, I could have went and did it, you know. But I went to be a RD ... recruit division commander. I had to. I asked for that billet 2 years before I got it. And every time I asked the detailer for it, he said "Well, we're not letting anybody out of the rate. You either have to go to the training facility, ah, the hailing facility, you know. You had to go to the same career path that everyone else was going. And I told him, you can't advance going the same places everyone else is going, because then you have to work that much harder to stand out, you know.

Master Chief James believes that during his time in the Navy, his achievements have made a difference and that the impact will be long-term. He discussed this impact and why he thinks it will be long-term:

> Going to Great Lakes and being a recruit division commander and taking responsibility for 94 civilians and turning them into sailors. That was the biggest thing. That was the biggest leadership challenge. That was the biggest personal challenge because I had to put aside ... I had to think about the fact that someone else is just starting out ... I think every sailor remembers that Chief who cared and who didn't care, you know. Because a Chief had to become that father figure and the individual kinda takes things from that figure. And hopefully, I have been able to give them some positive things and if I gave them some bad things, some negative things, hopefully they'll learn from those also and they won't do those things themselves.

In addition to believing he has made a long-term difference during his time in the Navy, Master Chief James also stated that there was nothing he did not accomplish that he wishes he had. He added:

> I haven't been in a position where I was totally disliked or frowned, I was totally frowned upon. It hasn't all been cherries and whipped cream. But it's definitely ... I've seen people ... I've seen some Chiefs, you know — African Americans, Caucasians — that just could not get going and the command

would not let them get going. They'd already made a preconceived judgment on these individuals and they were not meant to succeed. That was definitely one of the things that I learned at Great Lakes and dealing with the surface community. If you were in, you were in if things went wrong. If you weren't in, you were gonna stay right there until you went somewhere else. And I had never seen that before.

While he stated that he accomplished everything he wanted to accomplish, he did state that, given an opportunity, he would like to go back to a submarine and be Chief of the Boat (COB). He discussed why:

Because I do feel, again, right now I can tell you in those, ah, stations — either Bangor, Washington, or King's Bay, Georgia — right now there is no Black Chief of the ... African American Chief of the Boat. And there was one but he, ah, became ill. So right now, you've got ... say, 12 commands, ah, 10 maybe [where] junior individuals ... don't have a leadership figure that they can relate to, you know. And this guy's saying, "You're telling me to advance. You're telling me to do all these things. What do I see that this can come true?" They can't see it, you know. So I want to go back. If I had.... If I didn't pick up Warrant Officer, I would go back to a submarine — a sea-going vessel — to be Chief of the Boat so that they [African Americans] can see somebody. So they can see an African American in that position. And it's funny because though it happened before, I know now that to go back and be an African American Chief of the Boat, I would be on *All Hands Magazine*. I'd be in the little *Periscope Magazine*. And they'd make it seem as though it's something they'd never seen before. You know, it's, "Wow, you know, we just made an African American Chief of the Boat." And I'm like, man, why is that in a military that professes to be so diverse — and it probably is more diverse than a lot of companies — but to be as diverse as it professes to be, why is this still in this day and age something that makes us say "OH?" You know, shouldn't that just be a common occurrence? Shouldn't that be the norm? Shouldn't, shouldn't we accept that? I think so. But that's not the way it is.

Our conversation then shifted to Master Chief James's views and experiences with mentorship. I asked him if he had had any experiences with mentorship and, if so, to discuss those experiences. He responded,

The mentorship that I had at the time wasn't like you said, the documented formal mentorship, you know. It was a mentorship where I had that senior person, you know, like you said, was maybe directing me or guiding me and they didn't always sit there and tell me why or what the end goal was, you know. A lot of these individuals I probably didn't like at the time, you know. But then again a lot of people probably didn't like 'em. So I [was] probably kinda just on the bandwagon. Well, fortunately for me, the individual saw through that, you know. The mentorship program, like you said, right now is a big thing in the military. I try to sit down and talk with my Chiefs and talk with them and find out if I see a weak area, you know. What they need or where they need to grow ... maybe in time management ... leadership ... dealing with senior individuals — department heads, division officers. Not everyone does that, you know. For some people, that program ... mentorship is something that we have always done, so why do we need to put a tag on it now, a label on it and why do we need to document it? We've always done it. Well, because of that, because we didn't document it, because there is no tag on it, some people do it and some don't, you know. Some do it better than others. Right now, they got a program that is basically written out for you and tells you exactly what you need to do to help an individual progress, okay. I think a lot of times what we lose track of is when we talk about progressing, they're thinking advancement up through the ranks. Sometimes, progression can be a personal progression, you know. That individual can take some of the things they learn in dealing with people and situations and apply [them] to their civilian life and be better people, you know. I tell all my guys, not everyone's gonna do 20 years. Not everyone's gonna do 30 years. Not everyone's gonna make Chief, okay. But you are gonna be a man until the day you die, you know. So the things that you need to do to help you grow as an individual and if you grow as an individual and then if you choose to go on and make the military your career, you can do better at that and hopefully make better decisions in doing that later on.

I asked him to express his views on the quality of the mentorship he received and he discussed the shortcomings:

You know, I'd like to say that I wish someone had sit me down and talked to me and explained exactly what they were doing or what they expected of me, you know. That way it would have helped me. It would've gave me a better path, you know. Some people will tell you, "Hey, your career path has always been there. You know, it's always been E-3, E-4, you know, E-5, E-6, E-7 ... that's your path. That's your career path." But it would've helped if someone had said, "You know what, in order to reach that next level, do this. Do that. Have you thought about this? Do you know that this will do this to you." Finance. Ah, gosh, for the longest time, my finances were terrible. Because even though we had command financial specialists on the board, the only time we went to him was when we had a problem. If you didn't have a problem, no one said anything to you. So then you were left to believe that, "You know what, if I'm not having a problem, I'm doing okay." Well, that's not necessarily the truth all the time.

I asked him if he could compare the mentorship Black sailors received with that which White sailors received. He drew some stark differences:

I think the biggest difference was that White sailors can relate to the individual that was mentoring him because they had some commonality ... they saw a lot of the things the same way, you know. They hadn't seen any racial prejudice. And being that I was in a small division, I didn't see so much in my division but I do remember us going or pulling into a port and going somewhere and my LPO made a conscious effort to make sure I was accepted also.

And because of that, we didn't go to some places. Some clubs that maybe if they had went by themselves, then ... they didn't go because they wanted to make sure that I felt comfortable, you know. And I remember then thinking, "You know what, I really appreciate the fact that these guys did that for me." You know, so because of that, I think that made a big impact on me to do the same for other people. But I really appreciated the fact, you know, those Caucasian individuals—'cause they could have easily just left me and said, "Hey, fend for yourself" you know. "We're going to have a good time." Ah, but because of that, like I said, when they're talking to me, when they're making a kind of reference, they don't know what it's like to grow up ... some of them with a single parent, you know, father being an alcoholic mother working ... my mom worked in a shoe factory, you know, for a while before she went to clean apartments. They couldn't relate to that, to living with your grandmother, with your aunt, and your other cousins, you know, and your grandfather. So they, they didn't know, they didn't ... I didn't want for anything [while I was] coming up. Well, I didn't have all those things that they may have had, you know. So when it came to music, when it came to history, you know, we weren't on the same page.

As he began to discuss the role he believes race played in his career, Master Chief James stated that his experiences may be different from those experienced by other African American sailors. He then proceeded to discuss how he believes he has been "blessed." He continued,

I believe that I've been blessed to have supervisors, commanding officers, that didn't see that race. They judged me and they judged the sailors around me by their performance. You know, I'm sure you can probably talk to some sailors, maybe at different commands or may have worked for other people, that feel that they may have been fired or may not have been given an opportunity because of their race. But I didn't ... I never had a position like that. You know, like I say, I can only say that's a blessing it's there. They do have people out there, you know, that feel certain ways about certain things. I feel fortunate enough to have been in a direct situation while I was in the military where race was a ... a public issue, you know.

Although he does not believe race has disadvantaged him in any way throughout his career, he does believe that race has worked to his advantage. He provided an example of how this advantage may have been manifested:

I would like to say "yes" because sometimes I think because of my race, sometimes they may feel I don't know something that I do. Then, when I tell them that ... tell them what I know or show them or make something happen that they didn't think would happen, and now it gives me points, you know. Now they're, like, "Man, I need to reevaluate that because I may have sold him short in that area because of, you know, ah, his color. And now I see where he was quick on that. He was, able to make this happen. He was able to do this or do that." So in a way, that can play to your advantage.

He also discussed how he felt the need to be more well-rounded in order to fit in. He stated, "There are things I felt that I needed to know that they ... growing up, you know, [I] didn't watch the news as much as I do now." Additionally, he discussed how he perceives race affected his relationship with some of his White peers once he was promoted to Master Chief. When I asked him if he has been able to fit in, he stated,

> You know what, I don't think it's so much that I fit in. You know, or even [be accepted as] equal; like I said, in my job and in my rate there is like only one other African American E-9 and I can see and I've seen when I walk into the room and I know guys got animosity toward me because I made E-9 and they're still E-8 ... but the thing about it is now they're forced to accept me. You know, sometimes I'm kinda like, ... a smack in their face or, ... throwing water in their face because now they've gotta take it. They've gotta give me that respect. They've gotta give me the courtesy that the position has ... whether they want to or not.

As we talked about his competence and the degree to which his competence was accepted as equal to that of his White peers, Master Chief James discussed the phenomenon that many other African American men express — the belief that they worked harder than their White colleagues. He described this as he discussed the degree to which his competence was accepted as equal:

> It was, because when I was coming up through the ranks, say E-4 and E-5, you know, the individuals that I was coming up with, the Caucasian missile techs that I was going up through the ranks with, luckily my performance showed higher, or made me stand out a little more than theirs. And maybe that's because I had to work harder. Or maybe I'm not saying I had to work harder. I chose to work harder than maybe they did to make sure that I knew my job. Because they may have — and maybe some of this was perceived on my part — I believed that I had to know more; I had to do more in order to make sure that I didn't fail. I didn't want to give myself or give them the opportunity to put me in a position where I might fail. So because of that, I chose to study harder. I chose to make sure that I knew exactly what I was supposed to be doing when I went for that board or when I went to that, you know, that process or something so that there wouldn't be someone to catch me and [say] "See, I knew he wasn't gonna know that." I tried to prevent that. I tried to do everything I could to prevent that from happening.

I then steered our conversation to the topic of meritocracy and the military's claim that it has created, within American society, an organization where merit is the sole determinant of one's level of success. When I defined the term as such, Master Chief James responded,

> [sigh] You know what, it's, it's one of those things where you wish it was and I do believe that they are trying to get there. I do believe they're trying to get there and that is the intention of the military. But just this past Summer, in July, I went to the equal opportunity symposium that was held here at Patrick Air Force Base and of the 300-plus personnel there with equal opportunity, the majority, I mean clearly more so, the majority was not African American, you know. Mind you there we may have had ... I think it was seven E-9 African American males, you know. But that was right there for that and we were still the smaller number. I believe the military's ... we're trying. The Navy is trying to go that way but it's trying to be a, a company or a business that looks at the performance of the individual. I think what may be part of our problem is we have to get our members and our individuals to realize that they can and they should be awarded the opportunities to take these higher positions, you know, go and put in these packages ... I talked to an individual just last week and he was talking about how if you look at the military and see ... you look at the percentages across the board, ah, there may have been 87% [of the] minorities [who applied] that got picked up for the officer program and 87% [of the] Caucasians [who applied]. Well, the numbers, percentage numbers they show you doesn't tell you that there may have been 200 to 400 Caucasians that put in for that program of which say 87% got picked up and there may have only been 20 to 40 minorities that put in, of which, you know, say 87% got picked up. So you're looking at ... a lot of times we see the numbers that they want to portray that makes us look the best across the board. But if broken down at the actual numbers, we still aren't equal. You know, we don't have the same amount of people applying for those positions. We don't have the same amount going up for advancements. I do believe until you become eligible for E-7, you do get advanced, for the most part, based on your performance and that's basically being on a test, you know. The test isn't ... the test is color-blind. The same questions are available and are given to everyone, okay. But once you become a Chief, now you're being advanced, again on your ability, your performance, the job you've taken and how well you performed at your job.

As we wound up our conversation, I asked him for his views on the Navy's assertion that it has been a success story with integrating people of different backgrounds. He agreed that the services have done a good job and proceeded to point out some weaknesses:

> I think the military has done a good job of integrating, you know, and having personnel of different cultures, different races. But where I think our problems lie is where we try to ... where we have issues because of the fact that we don't understand or we haven't dealt with the ... we don't know where these folks are coming from. Ah, take for example, if you have this young African American third class petty officer who gets offended when the individual, you know, curses at him talks down to him, okay. Well, that Caucasian individual may feel, "Well, you know what? I talk to everyone that way. You know, and if I talk to everyone that way, you shouldn't be offended by it. Get over it."

Well, he may keep doing it because he feels that he's not doing anything wrong because he does that to everyone. And that African American youth may let him know, "You know what, I don't like that. I don't take that. Don't do it." And then eventually, he'll be looked at as the bad guy because that same guy can say the same thing to a young Caucasian, ah, sailor and that guy not get mad. So because the African American youth got mad, now he's the bad guy. So I think our biggest problem, our biggest, ah, gap is the understanding of cultures, you know.... When we were in boot camp it was that way because they had a hard time adapting, you know. Everyone wants discipline. But the type of discipline that was being given was harder for that African American youth to take than maybe it was for the Caucasian individual. And maybe that was because they knew, that Caucasian knew that it was a game and knew not to take it personally, you know. They know at the end of it, everything was going to be alright and we can all go, you know, get some coffee and it'll all be over with and it'll be something that we can talk about. And that African American youth took it offensive, you know. When you told him, "Hey, you know what, you better do this or I'm gonna kick your ass," they took for granted, "You know what, this individual's gonna try to kick my ass." You know they're going and preparing themselves to make sure this don't happen. Whereas the Caucasian youth knows, "Hey this is just something somebody's saying just to be saying it." So, yea, all the diversity that we have and the big mix or the big ... the things that the Navy has done to make it better, there are still steps that we can take to make it more well-rounded ... to make it more of success story for the African American youth. And the biggest part of that is understanding where he is coming from.

Master Chief James and each of the participants introduced in this chapter have provided their experiences through their own subjective lenses. It is from these subjectively reported experiences that one coherent storyline is derived that reflects the collective story provided by the participants. In the following chapters, this storyline is revealed, along with an analysis, conclusions, and recommendations for change.

4

Barriers to Full Inclusion

> *What the "good ol' boys' club" in my experience tends to be [is] the network of personal and social relationships that allowed people to receive opportunities, to receive information, allow people to connect to others that had the ability to assert some influence in decisions regarding their abilities to move.... I didn't know any African Americans that were key individuals in that good ol' boys' club.*
>
> — Chief Hines

In almost all areas of society, African American men continue to face barriers to full inclusion. From the corporate workplace to political office, African American men continue to find limitations on their access to positions of power and prestige. The literature shows that even in an area that has served as a vehicle toward a better life for many young African American men — the sports arena — these men remain largely sidelined from positions of leadership (Hill, 2006; Allen, 2006). While the private sector does not claim to have eliminated all barriers that are based on race, the military is often held as a model of a workplace where barriers based on race no longer exist.

Such claims are put forth even in the face of statistics that show large gaps in the achievement levels of African American men and their White male colleagues. Moreover, these claims have been advanced largely by those who have not existed as African American men within the military system. However, when provided an opportunity to offer their own views on this, African American men paint a far different image than that advanced by many scholars and the military itself. Many of these men, in reflecting on their own experiences, clearly identify what they see as barriers to full inclusion. In this chapter and those that follow, I have lifted themes from the preceding narratives, provided by the participants, to tell their collective story.

The Good Ol' Boys' Network

In the United States, the granting of career opportunities based on personal associations has historically been and currently remains a fact of life. The ability to create networks with those in positions of power and influence has largely become an expected competency of the upwardly mobile. In the civilian sector, the vast majority of those in positions of power and influence are White males. The impact that this has had on the ability of historically marginalized groups to make inroads into America's corporate boardrooms is reflected in the paucity of African American men and other minority groups in positions of power.

While these facts about private sector employment are fairly well known, that similar conditions exist within the military is not. However, the majority of those interviewed indicated that many career decisions are made based on personal associations. Phrases such as "the good ol' boy network" and "close to the throne" were frequently enunciated to describe the informal networks within the military that lead to what they perceive to be the unjust distribution of opportunities. Chief Hines describes with some resentment his experience in one of the Navy organizations in which he worked:

> Once I made it to Chief and considering all the off-duty education, I've done a lot of things. I also worked with some various platforms. I never received sailor of the quarter. I never received any of those accolades that others received ... who were primarily White. Once I made Chief, I enjoyed [a] tremendous degree of latitude, for the most part. Then, once I arrived at a submarine training center, I encountered what is commonly known as the "good ol' boys' club." If I didn't gain the acceptance of the Master Chief and Senior Chiefs in key leadership positions, most of whom were White, it was pretty much a conclusion that I would not see Senior Chief. Essentially, that is exactly what happens. The irony is that most that did were those that were able to socialize with, those that catered to, this group of people, those that golfed with this group of people, those that drank with this group of people, [they] were those that received the more career enhancing opportunities. I didn't do that because it was very distasteful to feel like I was being somebody's groupie. I figured that my mind, skills, personal abilities, and my competencies were equal to, if not exceeding, theirs.

The ability of corporate CEOs to create or end careers in short order is well known. Such power is often considered an entitlement of those who have managed to ascend the corporate ladder. However, in many ways, those in positions of leadership within the military exercise similar power over those who are in lower ranks or positions. Although the military's advancement and transfer systems are detailed in policies that are designed to govern the conditions under which service members are promoted and assigned, those in positions of power — much like corporate CEOs — often exert their influence to affect outcomes and often those decisions are based on personal associations. In chronicling one particularly callous display of power, Chief Hines recalls,

> What I mean is I was privy to some backroom dealings later on in my career where a group of Master Chiefs got together and I was there. It was a very informal setting, private party more or less. I had been asked to go along to drive a particular Master Chief who knew me well. I've worked with him and he'd been having heart problems and didn't need to be driving. He asked me if I would mind driving him over there. So for that reason I was there. I recall them discussing individuals who they thought needed to be promoted, who they thought needed certain orders. They were determining people's lives and careers over their beer and barbeque chicken. These people had no idea. I know of an individual that actually had orders; his household goods had been shipped; his family was prepared to go. They changed his orders right there and this guy was over in another country and had no idea what happened to him. I was thinking, that's going to be a real blow to him.

The military is replete with policies that govern the way business is supposed to be conducted. These facially neutral policies — if executed as written — may go far in removing barriers to opportunities for some, while also eliminating the unearned advantage that many receive due to their personal associations. However, there currently remains the real potential for policies to be overridden simply by those in positions of power exerting their influence. The result may be actions that effectively construct barriers that indirectly affect promotion opportunities for those who are not members of the in-group. One factor that has the real potential to affect advancement opportunities is the ability to attend military technical school.

While the Navy has some schools that are required for promotions, most technical schools are not required for promotion, but are designed to increase knowledge and competence. However, because they provide sailors with the requisite knowledge to do well on advancement examinations, these technical schools may directly impact promotion opportunities. Further, they often increase sailors' technical competence, making them more proficient in the performance of their duties. The result may be higher marks on performance evaluations, which play a major role in determining who is selected for promotions. Thus, manipulating the process by which these schools are assigned may have a real effect on sailors who may be disadvantaged. As described by Master Chief Ivans, this sometimes happens:

> So I wanted to go to be an expert satellite operator, one of the top schools for my rating we had got money for it. I was in line for it. We also needed a teletype repairman, so I was always the top communicator, ah, was doing the job without the training. The training would definitely help me promote. We got the money for the school. I always thought I was going, was never told otherwise. When it came time for the school date, they sent a White male and I didn't know anything right up to ... I always thought I was going. I requested the school numerous times. I was doing the job without the training, and then what was finally told to me when I put in a request to ask why I couldn't go was that I was doing a fine job without the training [and that] they wanted to train somebody else up to be able to work with me. So that person actually never really did the job. When they came back, they transferred and got a bonus because of the school ... what we call NECs. They show that you're qualified for the specialty. But I remained doing the job and this person got paid the bonus and never did the job and went on to another command.

Several of the respondents discussed incidents where they perceived the actions of military personnel in positions of authority to have disadvantaged them in favor of others with whom the senior personnel had personal associations. Many of the respondents' accounts involved situations where their promotions may have been directly affected by those actions, contradicting the view that the military is fully inclusive. Moreover, as is often the case in other contexts, the participants' accounts demonstrate how under-the-table deals are made and how those deals may have real impact on those who are not considered a part of the in-group.

The In-Group: A View from the Outside

All organizations have cultures that govern such things as patterns of behavior, dress, communication patterns, and other aspects of how the organization and those within it are to conduct themselves. Kotter and Heskett (1992) suggest that these cultures represent the "values that are shared by the people in a group and that tend to persist over time even when group membership changes" (p. 4). The ability of an employee to fit within an organization's culture is at least as important as technical competence. Accordingly, new employees are automatically encouraged to follow the patterns or styles that characterize an organization's culture (Kotter & Heskett, 1992). Those who are unable or unwilling to fit those non-skill-based patterns are likely to encounter barriers that have a real impact on their career mobility.

In the United States, the vast majority of corporations are created by White men and the organizational cultures are constructed to correspond with the values and tastes of those by and for whom the organizations were constructed. To those who fit within these cultures, they are invisible, "normal" ways of behaving. But for those who have different communication patterns, dress codes, and tastes, these cultures can present as difficult obstacles to overcome. As asserted by Feagin and Sikes (1994), "White workplaces rarely accommodate basic black interests and values. Instead, Black employees are expected to assimilate" (p. 163). Because the military has its own culture, a culture that, not unlike those in corporate America, was constructed by White men, African American men — who are often quite competent — sometimes find themselves struggling to achieve, in spite of their competence. Chief Andrews demonstrated this in his discussion of two equally deserving sailors:

> I've got a White female and a Black male sailor. Both of them work very hard and both of them are good sailors. However, the young Black male sailor has the perception that he's a thug. Part of it is his fault. When I say his fault [it's] because I've sat down and talked to him. I said, "You've got to understand there is a time and place for everything. When you hang out with your friends, you can speak that way. You can't carry that over when you're walking up and down the hallways or p-ways on the ship." Those same people see this female White sailor who every time they see her, she's speaking properly. She's addressing people. He's walking around singing rap songs, this, that, and the third. It's your own way of success. When I submitted these two names for quarterly awards, one — the White female — no problem, [they said] "Absolutely. She's great." The Black male sailor, they looked at me like, "You must be kidding. This guy is a thug. This guy is lazy. This guy is.... There is no way I would have this guy as representing the command." Yes, he warranted recognition but the perception by those that made the ultimate decision is what kept him from being awarded.... I feel that both sailors merit the recognition. However, because one is more acceptable.... It's very hard to overcome a perception one has of you, despite your efforts.

These young sailors, who are often 18 or 19 years old, find themselves in situations where they are confronted with the choice of either limiting their opportunities within the military or being considered sellouts by their friends. When asked why these sailors resist conforming, Chief Andrews responded,

> They don't want to be accused of selling out. I don't blame [them] for not wanting to sell out who they are. There's a compromise you have to make within yourself. At the same time, you're going to ask [them to be] somebody that's totally different from what they are. I don't want to change who I am just because my Chief thought I was a thug or my Chief thought just because I was a Black man that I didn't amount to nothing. I [don't] want to change who I am as a person, but strike a balance of keeping my individuality but prove I'm more than what you think I am.

Barriers to full inclusion are not only constructed based on how a sailor is perceived by the decision-makers. Some respondents in this study suggested that how they — as the sailors' Chiefs — are perceived by White leaders affects their sailors' careers. Because decisions on personnel actions, such as awards and discipline, are typically affected by the supervisor's credibility with the decision-makers, when African American Chiefs are not considered a part of the in-group, their sailors may suffer. Chief Butler discusses his experience with this:

> When I have to speak for somebody, I have to be dramatic. It has to have full impact for anybody to, to give any credit or validation to what I am saying. I can't simply come into a room and say, "This guy's doing well because he did this. Therefore I nominate him." If I did that, a lot of the people I represent would get jack. And I've seen it done. I've really seen it done. So, when it's time for those things, I really have to do homework and I have to practice what I'm gonna say to the rest of my brothers in the Chiefs' mess for impact. I have to be dramatic about it for them to get their fair shake.... My personal thought is I think they discredit a lot of things.... I'm saying because for some reason they may think that I'm not as smart as they are ... that my ability to evaluate somebody's performance is not as good as their ability to evaluate somebody's performance. That's what I think.

He continued by discussing how he was received by White Chiefs on selection boards when nominating African American or Latino sailors for awards:

> [B]ut if I'm putting up somebody Black or somebody Latino or something like that, I think ... they ... in my opinion, the first thing that comes to my mind is, "He just wants to get an award for another minority ... he just wants another minority to be sailor of the quarter." That's what I think. Because you can ... I can see the looks in their eyes when I mention the person's name. It's like they want to dismiss the entire thing as soon as I say their name.

Although African American Chiefs believe they were being scrutinized for nominating Black and Latino sailors for awards and other recognition, the majority of the respondents identified instances where they believed White sailors were given preferential treatment by White Chiefs. Senior Chief Gregg recounted a situation at one of his commands where Black sailors were being overlooked for training opportunities, in favor of White sailors. At that time, he was not a Chief, but he was the most senior African American in the organization and junior sailors complained to him about the preferential treatment. He recounts,

> I was the most senior Black person at one command and there were two or three junior White folks. And these other, all these other White folks were getting picked to train on the air traffic control equipment. A lot of the Black kids would come to me and say, "Hey, I don't know if you notice this, but I've been busting my butt studying. I've been busting my butt on this and this and they picked this person over me to do that." And I said, "Let me see what I can do" ... and I would talk to the Chief. I'd say, "Hey Chief, what's the deal? My man here was working hard and is he gonna get a shot?" And he'd go, "Oh yea, yea, his time is coming. His time is coming." You know, I'd say [to myself] "Okay. Well let's see how that goes." And his time didn't come. You know, the next thing you know, we're not at sea any more and you can't train if you're not at sea. And it was over with and I looked at that situation and was like, "That's messed up." So the guys ... you know, these three or four Black guys, you know they're junior but they're not getting a shot to do anything. And the only thing that turned things around was before we went on the next deployment, I was made the LPO, and in charge of all the radar stuff. So now that I'm in that position, I can go and get them trained. I was doing my best not to do it by race. I'm definitely trying to do it by merit, but I know these Black guys and I know how hard they worked. And I know how they just got looked over. I made sure that they got their shot.

Even achieving the most senior enlisted rank does not guarantee that African American sailors will be accepted on the "inside." The rank of Master Chief is a very prestigious rank within the naval service. However, Master Chief James demonstrated the difference between being accepted on the inside and being forced to accept his rank:

> You know what, I don't think it's so much that I fit in. You know, or even [be accepted as] equal; like I said, in my job and in my rate there is like only one other African American E-9 and I can see and I've seen when I walk into the room and I know guys got animosity toward me because I made E-9 and they're still E-8 ... but the thing about it is now they're forced to accept me. You know, sometimes I'm kinda like ... a smack in their face or ... the throwing water in their face because now they've gotta take it. They've gotta give me that respect. They've gotta give me the courtesy that the position has ... whether they want to or not.

The Exceptional Negro

One common practice in American society and in some organizations is to characterize African Americans who defy stereotypical preconceptions as being exceptions or unlike most Blacks. Such rationalization serves to defend the holders' faulty racialized views, which hold that all Blacks are alike. When they encounter some who are different from those preconceived notions, rather than reexamine their premise, they defend it through rationalization. A likely impact is the limiting of opportunities available to those who are not considered exceptions. It is not unreasonable to expect that if a Chief believes African American men are generally inferior, he would also expect that those men should not be working on multi-million-dollar radar systems. Only those who are "exceptional Blacks" should have those opportunities and be allowed on the inside. Senior Chief Gregg discussed his experiences with this phenomenon:

> Have you ever been in a situation — and I've been in these situations a whole bunch of times and I've been in these situations probably more times than I realize because people aren't saying it to my face. But on occasions I do hear them to my face and I've heard it after I left the military. It was ... "You know what, you really don't act like a Black guy. You don't act Black. You're not like the rest of them." Or something to that effect. At which point I get seriously offended.... I think a lot of times the expectation for me is ... for me, the expectation of White people ... of Blacks is that you're not intelligent. You're not sharp. So just like those four ... three or four Black guys ... they may not be able to handle the job, so let's go ahead and give it to somebody else. So when you encounter somebody who is intelligent that is Black, it kinda ticks 'em, you know it ticks 'em off. You know, it takes 'em off their game a little bit. On the other hand, it's hard to tell that person, "You can't do this. You can't do that" when you prove it to them on a regular basis. When you prove it to them so many times, they go, "You're just like one of us." No, I'm not...! To me, when they say that, that's their way of saying "We accept you." You know, "We'll accept you because you're kinda like our token Black...." I have to understand what it is [that I need to do] in order for me to be successful in this White male–dominated world. I know that once I cross the line of my culture as a Black male and come into this culture I cannot be exactly that. I'm still me. But I know that I need to talk the way you expect me to talk in order to be successful. If I talk the way you expect a Black person to talk, I would get exactly what you believe a Black person deserves, which is nothing.

Tokenism is common in many different settings in American life. Organizations often use this to draw attention to the *appearance* of progress in removing barriers for Blacks and other historically marginalized groups.

By publicizing the appointment of African American men to positions that have historically been denied to them, organizations may present such appointments as indications that they make appointments based on competence and that if other African Americans were as competent, they too could hold such important positions. The problem, it would seem, is that there are not enough who are competent. Adding to the discussion of tokenism, another respondent described it this way:

> I would go back to a submarine — a sea-going vessel — to be Chief of the Boat so that they [African Americans] can see somebody. So they can see an African American in that position. And it's funny because though it has happened before, I know now that to go back and be an African American Chief of the Boat, I would be on *All Hands Magazine*. I'd be in the *Navy Times*. I'd be in the little *Periscope Magazine*. And they'd make it seem as though it's something they'd never seen before. You know it's "Wow, you know, we just made an African American Chief of the Boat." And I'm like, man, why is it that in a military that professes to be so diverse — and it probably is more diverse than a lot of companies — but to be as diverse as it professes to be, why is this still in this day and age something that makes us say, "OH?" You know, shouldn't that just be a common occurrence? Shouldn't that be the norm? Shouldn't, shouldn't we accept that? I think so. But that's not the way it is.

While some of the respondents reported that they were viewed by some of their White military superiors and peers as being "different from other Blacks," the vast majority of those in the study felt that they did not feel pressures from the majority to change who they are — in terms of speech, associations, music, or dress — in order to fit in. Further, the majority stated that they were not concerned with fitting in. As stated by Master Chief Ivans,

> No, because I haven't tried to be accepted in a social function with White males. At work, I've always made sure if it's not offensive and it's within policy and standards and procedures of that organization, then individuals be able to be who they are and I'm able to be who I am. Ah, I can tell you, like dress codes for leaving the ... ship, I've seen that be in question because sometimes it seems like it's targeting a specific race.

Questioning Competence

In the Navy, those who ascend to the Chiefs' ranks are expected to be among the most competent in their respective fields. Because of the rigorous process of attaining this rank, such competence is generally assumed. However, nearly half of the respondents in this study indicated that their competence was not accepted as equal to that of their White male colleagues. Some discussed how their competence was outright dismissed by their White superiors. Senior Chief Gregg provided a vivid account of an incident where his superior officer, through his actions, dismissed his ability to perform his job:

> I would have to go brief the pilots and he would come with me to brief the pilots. He wasn't even supposed to be there. But then he was there. So I told 'em okay, this is what we're going to talk about, this is this, this is this, this is that. I told 'em about whatever is going on at the time. And I'd say, "What questions do you have for me?" The first person that would raise their hand, I'd go, "Okay, go ahead lieutenant." He'd ask me a question. As soon as I opened my mouth, my division officer answered the question. Somebody else asked another question. He answered that question too. He answered all the questions. I got nothing. I didn't answer a single question. I'm like, "What am I, his bodyguard standing there?" That's what it felt like. And I was like, I had never felt more inadequate. 'Cause I know they were looking at me awful, like "Why are you standing up here, Chief, if you're not going to answer any of these questions?"

The participants stated that while their competence is often challenged, similar challenges to the competence of White Chiefs are typically not made without cause and they are certainly not made because they are White. Although White Chiefs must give reason to believe they are incompetent in order for their competence to be called into question, African American Chiefs are often required to demonstrate their competence before being determined competent. As stated by one Chief, "My competence was challenged by my bosses, who believed I can't do as good as my White peers and that I had to show it to them. In showing it to them, [there] was too much work. I know what my job is. Just let me do my job." In discussing the differences in how competence is evaluated between Black and White Chiefs, Master Chief Ivans commented as follows:

> Not even graded on the same scale. In fact, if you're a White male—and I've worked for many—they'll tell you "I don't have a clue," but still get good reports and advance as high, up to par. [And they'll] take credit for your work. But [if] a Black male was to make that comment, they wouldn't last their tour of duty. And it's always challenged—your competence—because any little chance that someone can say that you may lack a little knowledge in an area, it's gonna be monitored closely to see if it's a, a glitch in your armor that can be penetrated.

Because they are aware of heightened scrutiny, African American Chiefs are generally careful to ensure they don't show a "glitch" in their armor. The majority of the respondents indicated that they went above and beyond to ensure they were good at their work. They studied hard and were proactive in seeking technical training to ensure they were competent in their field. Master Chief James, who believed his competence was accepted as equal to his White male colleagues, explained it this way:

> It was because when I was coming up through the ranks, say E-4 and E-5, you know, the individuals that I was coming up with — the Caucasian missile techs I was going up through the ranks with — luckily my performance showed higher, or made me stand out a little more than theirs. And maybe that's because I had to work harder ... or maybe I'm not saying I had to work harder. I chose to work harder than maybe they did to make sure I knew my job, because they may have ... and maybe some of this was preconceived on my part. I believed that I had to know more; I had to do more in order to make sure I didn't fail ... I chose to make sure that I knew exactly what I was supposed to be doing when I went for that board or when I went to that, you know, that process or something so that there wouldn't be someone to catch me and [say] "See I knew he wasn't gonna know that." I tried to prevent that. I tried to do everything I could to prevent that from happening.

A few of the respondents in the study cast these lowered expectations of competence in a more positive light. From their view, when Whites in positions of authority had lower expectations of Blacks' competence, it is easier to gain positive attention by meeting and exceeding their expectations. Master Chief James had such experiences and explained it this way:

> ... sometimes I think because of my race, sometimes they may feel I don't know something that I do. Then, when I tell them that ... tell them what I know or show them or make something happen that they didn't think would happen, and now it gives me points, you know. Now they're like "Man, I need to reevaluate that because I may have sold him short in that area because of, you know, ah, his color. And now I see where he was quick on that. He was able to make this happen. He was able to do this or do that." So in a way, that can play to your advantage.

Affirmative Action: Misperceptions of "Reverse Discrimination"

As in the greater society, misperceptions of how affirmative action programs are applied abound within the Navy. Such misperceptions breed contempt among colleagues, who believe some are given advantages in promotions based on race. These views are often used to justify why some Whites do not succeed and why some African American men do. Although the Navy does not give any special points or consideration for race at the point of selection for any of its pay grades, this fact is either not widely known or is disregarded. Even among senior enlisted African Americans, the view that the Navy has quotas for African Americans and other historically marginalized groups still exists. As demonstrated in the discussion above, it causes some African Americans to doubt that they were selected because they are equally competent as Whites who were selected. Such doubt based on faulty information also leaves Whites with this false sense of intellectual superiority and may create an undiscussed tension between African American males and their White colleagues. Discussing the role race played in his promotions, Chief Butler, who expressed strong confidence in his own competence, explained:

> I think it has played some role in my advancement. I think ... as far as making Chief, it has. I can't say this for certain, because I don't know as much about, ah, equal opportunity programs as I probably should, but I'm almost certain that there is a quota of what type of people that they're supposed to select. They're supposed to select so many Pacific Islanders; they're suppose to select so many African Americans and females and, you know, Hispanics and so forth and so on. So do I think it has had some impact? Of course I do. I think my record already spoke for itself, but for me to be Black and to be ... and to have all the checks in the block that they were looking for, it was perfect.

Even at the Master Chief level, there is misinformation about the issue of affirmative action within the Navy. Master Chief James discussed his own misinformed views about affirmative action and the process by which he became more informed:

> I used to believe ... I was one of those that believed, when I first made it, you know what, they had to make me because I was African American and they gotta make a quota. They've gotta make so many of us, you know. They gotta make so many Hispanics. They gotta make so many, you know of this. I believed that up until I sat the board myself this time. And when I sat the board, not once did anyone ask what anyone's race was while we were making our decisions as to who was qualified or who should be selected. When, of course, I'm sure when they broke up the demographics on the computer, that had all that on there ... but not once did we consider that when we were making the selections ourselves. So that was a good thing. That sorta made me feel, "You know what, I did truly make it off of my merit alone and it's the thing that did it and it had nothing to do with the fact that I'm African American and the fact that they had a quota." And unless they change it this board, like I said, I saw no pictures and I saw nothing in it that said they were trying to meet a quota when we made our selection.

In his discussion, he illuminated the impact the misinformation had on him and how becoming more informed caused him to feel proud of knowing that he achieved his rank on his own merit. Moreover, he provided some insight into how misinformation affected his White colleagues' opinion of him:

> You know what though, the thing with that, the sad thing with that though, it's not so much, I really didn't see so much with the African Americans, but I saw it more with my Caucasian counterparts. You can tell sometimes ... you can hear it behind your back or whatever. "Oh they made him ... they had to make him, you know, because you know they had to make so many...." They were using it as, like, a reason why ... I was being selected each time I went up, you know. A lot of these guys — because I went from West Coast to East Coast — a lot of 'em had no idea who I was anyway. They couldn't even tell you who I was, you know. But they figure when they saw that I was African American, "Oh well, they had to make him." You know, they knew, they know Jim Bob or Billy Bob who had been in this program for so long, you know. [So they would feel that] he's the one. They should make him because he's been the squadron guy or he's been this. They have no idea what my career path has been like ... the jobs I've taken on or how I had did while in those jobs. They just took for granted that because I'm African American, the reason I made it is because they had to make so many. And I do believe that because I've heard it from someone that they told it to who may have confided in me and believe that's what they did. So it was interesting on that side.

Limited Black Role Models

Members of groups that have been historically marginalized in society need role models of their own race to demonstrate to them that they too can succeed. As in American society at large, where African Americans are more heavily represented in some fields and are largely absent from others, there are many specialties in the military services where African Americans are very few in numbers. White Americans, who are of course amply represented in all career fields, both inside and outside the military, may not recognize the importance of individuals' seeing people who bear their skin color in positions of prestige and influence.

Although there are no policies that specifically exclude African Americans, the fact remains that in some of the electronics fields, some of the submarine-specific ratings, and aviation ratings, senior African American sailors are represented in very low numbers. One impact of having such low representation of African Americans and other underrepresented groups within a command is the decreased level of sensitivity of Whites to issues of race. Feeling less constrained, those who are so inclined may use disparaging remarks that cause the few African Americans within the organization to feel alienated. Such comments, which might not have been said if a critical mass of African Americans were present, may also offend Whites who must listen. Although these comments may not be intended to be harmful but rather are used as light-hearted jokes, they may offend the few African Americans, who may already feel isolated. Master Chief Ivans discussed such an incident where those comments came from the commanding officer — the senior person in the organization:

> So we're in a meeting talking about how we were gonna be paired up for the big inspection, and they were having problems with one of the leading firefighters on the ship and he was a Black male. And again, that same engineman said "Ah, we'll replace him." He was always thinking about "we'll fire" a person. And we were looking at other ways to do it. And so I recommended, pull him to the side and let him know how important he was to the team and to see how that would work. And the captain said he loved the idea. And he told me "I'm glad we got you onboard because you're the H-N-I-C." And then everybody laughed and I didn't think it was funny. Okay, so everybody laughed and I [don't] think they took it to mean anything. So after the meeting, I stayed back and I asked the captain what did that mean. And he laughed and he said "Chief" — I was a Chief at the time — he said "Chief, you've heard that before." And then I said "No, captain, I'm not sure that I have. Ah, you used some acronyms. What does that mean?" And then he told me that means, ah, "You're the head ... you're the head Black man in charge." And I said "Sir, but that's not the initials that's H-N-I-C." And he said "Chief, that's a compliment. Don't turn something and make it be something that it is not." I said, "But sir, that's offensive to me. If you thought that I said something that was in agreement with you, I would hope that you would not use that type of acronym in regards to me again." And he said, "Aw, loosen up, loosen up. We're all stressed because we got a big inspection. The other Chiefs knew exactly what I was saying." And I said, "Like I said again, captain, I didn't consider it to be funny and I would not like to be referred [to] that way." And he said, "Point was taken."

In that scenario, the most senior person on the ship made a comment in the presence of an audience that had only one African American present and apparently thought it was okay to do so. Because the African American was a Chief and had enough experience to know that he was within his rights to challenge the commanding officer on this, the captain was corrected. However, in situations where the sole African American is a more junior sailor, it is much less likely that such behavior would be challenged. Chief Hines discussed such an example:

> Sometimes it's hard to say because there is no empirical evidence. I was in the training session in the department I was in and the officer told a joke in training. He said, "What did Abraham Lincoln say after the three-day drunk?" I didn't know and a lot of the others didn't know. A Senior Chief in the back who hung a Confederate flag — and what the Confederate flag symbolized to me unequivocally at the time was someone that probably had racist tendencies — he stood up in the back and said, "I did what? I freed who?" ... The gentleman next to me, another Black male, just busted out laughing. I remember turning to him and saying "What the blank are you laughing about, man? The joke is about us being free."

Although these behaviors may appear harmless, military workplaces where racial epithets are used create hostile environments for African Americans, even when they are not used with malice. And in environments where Blacks are very few in numbers, such epithets and slurs may be more harmful.

5

Mentorship

> *How do you think I got a lot of this knowledge? I had mentors throughout my life that passed on that knowledge and I learned from it. So whatever is passed on to me, I give to them. You know, to the youth today or to anyone who wants to listen. You know, I will talk and tell you what I know if you'll listen.*
>
> — Senior Chief Evanston

It is well known in corporate America that effective mentorship is critical to upward mobility. The literature identifies specific functions of the mentor-protégé relationship. These include coaching, visibility and exposure, protection, sponsorship, and providing challenging assignments (Kram, 1985). These functions are important to career development and the mentor-protégé relationships serve to help facilitate this development. Further, recommendations and solutions generated by mentors must be applied and implemented in a social context (Mumford, et al., 2000). Thus, significant differences based on race and culture can inhibit the effectiveness of these relationships. Moreover, since the power brokers in society have traditionally been, and continue to be, White males, African American men have often been relegated to receive mentorship from those who have limited access to power.

Just as mentorship is important in the private sector, it serves many of the same functions within the military. The Navy's formal mentorship program was mandated by the Chief of Naval Operations in 2003. However, forms of mentorship far predate this mandate. Currently, many questions remain about the status of Navy mentorship before and after the 2003 decree. How do African American Navy men view the quality of their mentorship? Did they receive mentorship prior to the 2003 order? Do they view the quality of their mentorship to be equal to that of White sailors? Do they view it as important to their careers? Each of these questions about mentorship is important to understanding the barriers African American military men face and how they cope.

The Navy's Formal Mentorship Program

Mentors play an important role in the career of military personnel. In helping sailors chart their career paths, providing guidance on personnel issues, and giving feedback on appropriate behaviors, mentors serve much the same function as they do in the private sector. As in the private sector, access to suitable mentors is important to the effectiveness of the mentor-protégé relationship. Moreover, while mentors have been required for all personnel by Navy policy since 2003, some participants in this study stated that either they had never heard of the program before their current Navy organization or their organization had not started the program. Chief Andrews' description of many of the young African Americans who enter the Navy provides a clear understanding of why mentors are needed:

> You got kids that are ... like I said nobody joins the military to get kicked out or go UA or do anything that's going ... I don't know of any sailor that I've ever talked to when they first come in the military that have goals of getting kicked out of the military. So you've got good kids being kicked out. You got kids that got the potential but aren't being considered or be taken considered that they got something to bring to the table. If you tell me I'm a dirt bag enough times I'm either going to make you right or use that as fuel into the opposite. If you don't have people in your corner to guide you through those steps then you're just going to say, "Well shit, he's calling me a dirt bag all these times. I guess I am a dirt bag; I guess I'm a thug." So since I'm a thug let me go smoke some weed; let me go knock over a liquor store. Let me go [do] this or let me go do that." I know I'm going extreme in [this] example but I see it, especially on a ship my size. You see that a lot more commonly than you do in a smaller command or smaller division.

The majority of those asked had not been the protégé in a formal mentor-protégé relationship within the Navy. When asked about his experiences with formal mentors, one participant stated, "We had ... that's, that's policy now. That's everywhere. Yea, I have one ... I have someone's name on a piece of paper." This statement characterized the experiences of the majority in the study. Most clearly believe the Navy's current formal mentorship program lacks the requisite robustness to fulfill the mentorship needs of African American males. Few stated they had seen the fruit of a successful formal mentorship program. As Master Chief Ivans put it,

> And what we did, everybody was appointed a mentor in writing but nothing ... nothing really evolved around it. It was just that I could see that this person had a mentor. And it was still up to ... because that was mentioned within the command that a mentorship should be a mutual relationship, it should be driven by formal guidance. So it was put in writing, but I didn't see where a lot of mentorship, ah, evolved from that putting it in writing.

Just as the majority of the participants expressed the collective view that mentorship is critical to success in the Navy context, not having a mentor places sailors at a distinct disadvantage. This is especially true of African American male sailors who must navigate a system that was not designed with them in mind. Not having mentors to perform the functions that help these sailors adjust to and appropriately behave within the military structure often contributes to disciplinary problems that limit achievement.

Additionally, mentors help military personnel, who must adapt to this new and often very different environment, interpret the behaviors of those who are placed as supervisors over them. This is a critical component of survival in military environments. Failure to correctly interpret these managerial cues can lead, and often does lead, to inappropriate responses. Such inappropriate responses can ruin a career and have other long-term consequences. In such situations, military personnel often find themselves receiving discharges that are characterized as "other than honorable," "dishonorable," or "bad conduct" discharges. In some cases, these discharges may follow them into their civilian lives and affect their ability to vote, obtain federal or state jobs, or receive any military benefits to which they would have otherwise been entitled.

Moreover, many sailors who enter the Navy have never lived away from home and come at a very young age. Thus, many require mentorship to help them understand what is expected of them as young adults and with financial and other issues. Master Chief James discusses his own experiences as a young African American sailor:

> You know, I'd like to say that I wish someone had sit me down and talked to me and explained exactly what they were doing or what they expected of me, you know. That way it would have helped me. It would've gave me a better path, you know. Some people will tell you, "Hey, your career path has always been there. You know, it's always been E-3, E-4, you know, E-5, E-6,

E-7 ... that's your path. That's your career path." But it would've helped if someone had said, "You know what, in order to reach that next level, do this. Do that. Have you thought about this? Do you know that this will do this to you." Finance. Ah, gosh, for the longest time, my finances were terrible. Because even though we had command financial specialists on the board, the only time we went to him was when we had a problem. If you didn't have a problem, no one said anything to you. So then you were left to believe that, "You know what, if I'm not having a problem, I'm doing okay." Well, that's not necessarily the truth all the time.

Many White Chiefs do show interest in the development of junior African American male sailors. However, because recommendations and solutions generated by mentors must be applied and implemented in a social context, those sailors are often unable to make effective use of these interracial mentor-protégé relationships (Mumford, et al., 2000). Discussing some differences between the mentorship received by White sailors and Black sailors, Master Chief James highlights this point:

> I think the biggest difference was that White sailors can relate to the individual that was mentoring him because they had some commonality ... they saw a lot of the things the same way, you know. They hadn't seen any racial prejudice. And being that I was in a small division, I didn't see so much in my division but I do remember us going or pulling into a port and going somewhere and my LPO made a conscious effort to make sure I was accepted also. And because of that, we didn't go to some places. Some clubs that maybe if they had went by themselves, then ... they didn't go because they wanted to make sure that I felt comfortable, you know. And I remember then thinking, "You know what, I really appreciate the fact that these guys did that for me." You know, so because of that, I think that made a big impact on me to do the same for other people. But I really appreciated the fact, you know, those Caucasian individuals —'cause they could have easily just left me and said, "Hey, fend for yourself" you know. "We're going to have a good time." Ah, but because of that, like I said, when they're talking to me, when they're making a kind of reference ... they don't know what it's like to grow up ... some of them with a single parent, you know, father being an alcoholic, mother working ... my mom worked in a shoe factory, you know, for a while before she went to clean apartments.... They couldn't relate to that ... living with your grandmother, with your aunt, and your other cousins, you know, and your grandfather. So they, they didn't know, they didn't ... I didn't want for anything [while I was] coming up. Well, I didn't have all those things that they may have had, you know. So when it came to music, when it came to history, you know, we weren't on the same page.

Effective mentorship may serve as an important means of helping these young African American males appropriately interpret these cues they receive from their military supervisors. The majority of those in the study found that the Navy's formal mentorship program was not effectively fulfilling this role.

Informal Mentorship

Although the majority of those in the study had not been protégés in effective formal mentorship programs, most stated they had received informal mentorship and that this informal mentor was important to their careers. In fact, many had never even used the term "mentor." However, looking back, they saw that those informal mentors served important roles. Chief Andrews explains:

> I never used the word "mentor" until I came to my current command. This was the first command where we had a mentor program in writing. So it was folks that I naturally gravitated to. Over time I looked back and said, "Okay that person was my mentor; Senior Chief so and so was a mentor to me." Where I'm currently stationed is really where they had a mentor program and used that word. I had never used that word before now..... I tell folks one of the most influential mentors that I had was not someone that was on my job. I think it's important to have someone removed from your day to day grind that can give you a point of view on life, building relationships (professional & personal), and personal development. I owe my own successes in the Navy to those folks that helped me. Who took the time to say "This kid has some potential; let me see what I can do to keep him from going down the wrong path."

One might ask why it was necessary for the Navy to create formal mentorship programs if these informal mentor-protégé relationships were so successful. However, there are some good reasons to institute formal mentorship programs. Chief James explained the difference between formal and informal mentors and why effective formal mentorship programs are important:

> The mentorship that I had at the time wasn't like you said, the documented formal mentorship, you know. It was a mentorship where I had that senior person, you know, like you said, was maybe directing me or guiding me and they didn't always sit there and tell me why or what the end goal was, you know. A lot of these individuals I probably didn't like at the time, you know. But then again a lot of people probably didn't like 'em. So I [was] probably kinda just on the bandwagon. Well, fortunately for me, the individual saw through that, you know. The mentorship program, like you said, right now is a big thing in the military. I try to sit down and talk with my Chiefs and talk with them and find out if I see a weak area, you know. What they need or where they need to grow ... maybe in time management ... leadership dealing

with senior individuals — department heads, division officers. Not everyone does that, you know. For some people, that program ... mentorship is something that we have always done, so why do we need to put a tag on it now, a label on it and why do we need to document it? We've always done it. Well, because of that, because we didn't document it, because there is no tag on it, some people do it and some don't, you know. Some do it better than others.

Discussing his experience with informal mentors, Master Chief Ivans recounted,

So I can only say I really had one person that I ever ... I can call an informal mentor. And that person told me the potential they saw in me ... my abilities ... skills and abilities. [He] gave me books to read on how to develop the weaknesses that he identified in me. He challenged me on the hard stuff when he felt as though my ... the conduct or the example I was setting was not to the standard that he thought it should be for me. Ah, from the day he retired, he kept in contact with me and always asked what was my next endeavor, what was my next goal, how I was looking at attaining it, and what he could do to help me do that ... to achieve it. He would put me in contact with other individuals that, ah, in the military that could help me in that endeavor ... that have been down that road. So I just felt he took my best interest at hand from professionally to personally. So he really helped me to prosper.

His informal mentor performed many of the functions of a mentor identified by Kram (1985), such as coaching, visibility and exposure, protection, sponsorship, and providing challenging assignments. Further, because he was an African American male, the mentor was better situated to understand the very unique experiences of African American men in predominantly White organizations. In addition to fulfilling the important mentor roles identified above, these informal African American male mentors also modeled behaviors that were appropriate for the Navy workplace. This is particularly important for African American men. While examples of appropriate behaviors are important for protégés in general, for African American men demonstrations of how to appropriately and effectively work within a system that was not designed for them, and in which they are a minority, serve an especially critical function. Several respondents made reference to the importance of this modeling.

Study participants also noted a difference in the quality of the mentorship they received when compared to that received by their White colleagues. The majority of the participants in the study thought that Whites received more or better mentorship. However, they understood these differences in quality in different ways. While some saw the difference as being the ability of White sailors to more closely identify with their mentors, others defined the difference as favoritism. For example, one participant stated, "I think the biggest difference was that White sailors can relate to the individual that was mentoring him because they had some commonality. They hadn't seen racial prejudice." While in this case, the difference was articulated as being based on life experience, others discussed deliberate discrimination. Master Chief Ivans explains,

> A White sailor gets a mentor, from my observation, the day he walks onboard ship or the day they get to their first command in the Navy. And they're passed on [to] each command. It's ... they're called ahead and set up with somebody else to take that person on from that command. It's like ... it's always been an informal ... informal mentor program for White males ... and even White females are taken care of the same. If you're a Black male, it's just by the luck of the draw that you'll find someone who will take you ... ah, take interest in you and your career endeavor. Because a lot of the black males in the Navy that I have encountered, they never had a mentor so they never knew the importance of it.

Whether the differences exist because of the ease with which White protégés identify with their mentors, or they exist due to favoritism, the effect is to create a disparity in the quality of the mentorship that is largely based on race. Thus, many in the study consider it to be the duty of African American Chiefs to learn what they need to know in order to be good mentors for junior African American sailors.

The participants in the study clearly presented their collective view that mentorship is critical to succeeding in the Navy. The overwhelming majority received mentorship, of some kind, that they believed proved instrumental in their success. Further, they believe that there is a real disparity in the overall quality of the mentorship African American males receive, when compared with that received by their White male colleagues. Thus, it necessarily follows that, in their collective view, the absence of equal access to quality mentors creates barriers for African American men in their efforts to close the achievement gap between White males and themselves.

6

Meritocracy or Myth of Meritocracy?

> *I don't think it will ever be ... a system that is based strictly on merit unless you find a way to strictly eliminate the human factor. If there are people involved, then, then it's a dynamic where anything can happen.*
> — Senior Chief Gregg

Unlike other segments of American life, the military makes bold claims about having created, within American society, an organization where merit is the sole determinant of success. Additionally, the literature asserts this and many in society take it for granted. Such claims are made in spite of military statistics that show that African American men are more likely to enter into the military justice system as defendants, are less likely to ascend to the more senior enlisted and officer ranks, are more likely to receive negative discharges, and comprise the majority of those on the military's death row. While these claims are made by Whites within the military and some scholars, when faced with a definition of meritocracy that means the only thing that matters in determining success is one's merit, the participants in this study unanimously reject the view that the military has created a pure meritocracy. Although those who have not historically been the victims of widespread discrimination may be quick to label the military as a purely merit-based organization, those African American men who must live within the system tell a different story. As articulated by Senior Chief Evanston,

> That's, that's what they claim, and like I said, to a certain degree it's true. But that system, you have to understand, that system, all things being equal, would work, but there's one factor in that that makes it imperfect, and that's

people. Everybody thinks about things differently. People with their own agendas, you know, hidden agendas; people with their own prejudices; people with their own partiality; you know, those things always play a factor ... not always play a factor, but play a factor in a lot of cases. And as long as they do, that form of recognition is always going to be flawed.

Chiefs are often in positions where they are charged with making decisions that affect the lives of those who are subordinate to them. When these decisions are not made based on merit, the careers of sailors can be greatly affected. Offering a view from inside these decision-making bodies, Chief Hines responded to the assertion that the Navy has created a meritocracy:

> I totally disagree. I think that there are pockets and places where there are people that are conscientious and do strive for the meritocracy. I think that organizationally, that does not hold true. I've seen too many people receive opportunities, receive accolades, receive awards, receive rewards that they simply didn't deserve. I've seen people receive stuff just because it was somebody's turn so it might as well be this individual over here. I don't see meritocracy. I've sat on boards that were supposed to observe the merits of people, yet they were totally subversive in how they chose people for advancement, how to choose people for ranking, and to try to challenge it was almost like mutiny. [They would say] "This is the way we're going to do it. I know that's what that says, but this is my Chief's mess and this is how it's going to be." It was not based on merit. It was not based on merit.... Sometimes, I've seen commands go out of their way to take someone who was an African American or Hispanic and was determined to make them the top-performing sailor, which denied others a fair opportunity and some of those others were White. So that's not what represents meritocracy either.

The Navy has promulgated policies that prohibit discrimination based on non-merit factors such as race. However, other factors that are often aligned with race may create outcomes that equate to race. For example, when decisions are made based on how much the supervisor has in common with particular people and the supervisor tends to have more in common with those of his or her own race, the outcome then becomes racially significant. Moreover, since common interests represent a non-merit factor, it in and of itself runs counter to the tenets of a meritocracy. Those in the study provided discussions of numerous situations that they say were based solely or in part on race. Some of these involved decisions about living conditions, job assignments, autonomy, and awards. In discussing a situation relating to bias in determining living conditions, Chief Hines stated,

> I had an incident when I was on a particular ship. When they assigned berthing, it turns out they assigned all the minorities to a certain berthing area, and all of the Whites to a more desirable berthing area. This was in the medical department.... I do [believe assignments were deliberately made based on race]. I do in that particular department because we have control over how we assign the people that come to our department. It's more ironic that everyone that was a minority, everyone that was but Deb. By Deb, I mean, we had a bright young man that has an obvious drug addiction. He had been through non-judicial punishment several times. So he was put down there, but everyone else — Hispanics, Blacks — that's where they were. Everyone White was placed up in this other more desirable berthing. This occurred over a period of time. Whether it was consciously done, I can't say. But the fact is that it happens and that's the way it was.

While decisions about where one lives on a ship are important to those who must live there, and in this case may be indicative of supervisors' views on issues like race, the impact is not normally far-reaching and typically has little or no impact on one's promotion opportunities. However, military job assignments may have a major impact on promotions, and some of the participants in this study discussed situations where they believe job assignments were made based on favoritism, at least, and possibly race. Discussing what occurred between him and one of his White peers, Master Chief Ivans discusses this issue:

> Me and him came in the Navy at the same time, within one week of one another. He had the opportunity the same as I did — but I wasn't planning on staying in — to be accelerated advanced to Petty Officer Third Class. I decided not to take it because I was not gonna stay in the Navy. We did the same thing. Once he got to the ship and I was doing better than him and so forth and I was gonna be the next duty radioman, the Senior Chief went down — at first talked to him — went down to [the] personnel [office], they backdated all his records and said that he wanted to be a petty officer. They gave him back pay, made him a Petty Officer and then put him in the section with me, for me to work for him when he wasn't even qualified for the job. So he was the Petty Officer. I was qualified and I worked for him. So I knew definitely race played into that. He didn't want me to be a Black seaman as the duty radioman.

In spite of the military's policies, those in positions of power retain the ability to affect who gets what jobs. This Chief discussed how someone in a position of power can use influence to manipulate the system and create outcomes that place one sailor above another. Similarly, the level of autonomy that is granted — which has the potential to have a real impact on careers — is determined by those in positions of power. When those decisions about who gets how much autonomy are made based on non-merit factors, the organization cannot be considered a meritocracy. Because of its rigid hierarchical structure, the military is exceptionally prone to this problem. In many cases, those who are only one pay grade higher are in a position to determine the degree of autonomy granted to subordinate sailors. The opportunity for a misuse of power is an ever-present reality. Even Chiefs—who are recognized experts in their fields and are often referred to as the backbone of the Navy—are subject to restrictions of autonomy to an extent that is determined by the officers appointed over them. In many cases, the Chief is significantly more experienced than the officer appointed over him. Senior Chief Gregg discussed how his autonomy was restricted by a commander for reasons that he believed were not based on merit:

> You know, this wasn't my first ship, so I knew what I had to do. But he was just, "don't do it." So anytime, you know, some serious situation came up, he just tried to bowl me over. [He would say], "We're gonna do it this way." I'm like, "Commander, the books says we have to do it this way; we're gonna do it this way." You know, he'd say, "Are you arguing with me?" [I would say], "No sir, I'm not arguing with you. We'll do it your way." Until we came to heads one day when it just became real ugly when I told him, "I don't give a damn what you do to me after I'm done with this job, but I'm gonna do it this way ... whether you like it or not."

This Chief, an expert in his field, had not been allowed to demonstrate his skill in that particular organization. Perhaps, such withholding of autonomy could be explained if the sailor was more junior in rank. However, the Navy grants prestige to those in the Chief's ranks because of their technical and managerial expertise and their years of service. In withholding the authority of the Chief to perform the job that he was assigned and which was well within his expertise, the commander may well have been acting based on a non-merit factor. The impact of this inability to have sufficient autonomy to perform could reflect in the Chief's evaluation and impact on his promotion to the next higher grade.

Several respondents pointed to the distribution of awards as another non-merit factor that impacts the careers of African American men. In the Navy, awards are often looked upon favorably when making decisions about advancement. In the lower ranks, some awards add points to the final multiple that determines who, among those who passed the advancement examinations, are selected for promotion. In the senior enlisted ranks, some of these awards are considered favorably when decisions are made concerning who is selected for Chief, Senior Chief, or Master Chief. For example, the person who is selected as Sailor of the Year competes at different levels and, if this person is a First Class Petty Officer, could potentially be meritoriously promoted to Chief by the Chief of Naval Operations. This is one of the very few awards that could result in such promotion. The initial decisions about who is recommended for awards are typically subjectively made by the sailor's Chief or leading Petty Officer and, because they are subjective, sometimes the most deserving are not the ones chosen. Master Chief Ivans discusses it as follows:

> The first person I can say that really had a big impact on me and the way that I looked at the Navy, it was a White Master Chief. Ah, at first, I took it as though he had an interest in ... my best interest because I was just learning about the military. But as time developed — this is my opinion of him — he would select certain minorities.... He would, like, give you what I considered bennies for a selective period so it wouldn't bring any highlight on what his whole intentions were, [which] was to hold other minorities back. So if you were new at a command, he would identify with some of your strengths and some of the abilities you had, but when it came time for Sailor of the Year or when it came time to put someone in for an award, it went back to the same, regime that I had saw at sea. It was even going on on shore duty.... Specific example, I was ranked [the] number one First Class but when it came time for Sailor of the Year, ah, it was always mentioned what I could do more of. But then that's what I targeted on to say, awards are subjective.... And I noticed that with him, when it came time for that, he would only focus on my negatives.

The looseness of the awards nomination process leaves major loopholes that allow those who are not truly committed to the tenets of equal opportunity to manifest their bias. Here, again, those in positions of power can and do exert their influence to manipulate the system. Senior Chief Gregg described a situation that happened to him:

> When I left [the command], they said, "Okay, we're gonna give you the Navy Achievement Medal when you leave. So I left there. I got to my new duty station, I'm like, "Okay, where's the medal. The medal is supposed to come." You know, the paper work was a little slow. It's supposed to come. When I called back to Personnel, [I] said, "Hey, I'm suppose to get a Navy Achievement Medal and I'm wondering what's the hold up? Is the write-up wrong and had to be redone or something? What's going on?" He goes, "Oh no, maybe about a month after you left, they ... your division officer just pulled that medal" ... he said, "Oh yea, he came down here and did it himself. He just withdrew it." I said, "Wow." He couldn't do anything to my face, but behind my back this is what he did.

The participants in the study raised another issue that sometimes arises within organizations and inhibits the creation of a pure meritocracy.

Recognizing the presence of barriers to the full inclusion of African Americans and other traditionally marginalized groups, some within organizations act based on non-merit factors to advance the careers of members of those underrepresented groups. Although they view such actions as warranted proactive measures to overcome the effects of systemic and past discrimination, those actions can run counter to the tenets of meritocracy. Discussing this issue, Chief Hines posited,

> There are often times that I would tell them if they're insistent on the fact that it is a meritocracy, they can accept that perhaps there are some shortcomings in the system. I have to tell them they are operating in a vacuum or their ability to perceive is so limited, or they are unwilling to acknowledge to themselves because they may have to incriminate themselves in creating or perpetuating that system. The fact is there's not a total inclusive meritocracy for everyone that's a part of the organization. Sometimes I've seen commands go out of their way to take someone who was an African American or Hispanic and was determined to make them the top performing sailor, which denied others a fair opportunity and some of those others were White. So that's not what represents a meritocracy either.

This issue, perhaps more than others, brings into clear focus the complexity surrounding the issue of creating a pure meritocracy. It raises the question: "How does one get beyond race without first taking account of race?" Even if—and that's a really major "if"—the military could eliminate the individual bias of its members and address the other existing barriers, the system would start with White males having an unearned advantage. The Navy has—as has society at large—through its actions, created a situation where African American men and others have been excluded, discriminated against, and marginalized through actions that had nothing to do with merit. The result of this is a huge gap in the achievement level between the marginalized and those who received unearned advantage. This is reflected in the near absence of African Americans in the aviation fields, certain submarine fields, certain technology fields, and the most senior officer ranks.

In supporting its claim of meritocracy, the military points to its success at integrating people from all races, sexes, and backgrounds. Although each of the participants in this study agrees that the military has generally been successful in integrating people of different backgrounds, most expressed concerns about the quality of the integration. For example, several suggested that the military, in its integration efforts, has failed to foster cultural understanding among the groups. As articulated by Senior Chief Gregg,

You know, the military, they are ... they're pretty good at putting a lot of people together. They're not very good at helping people understand one another. Just because ... because to me, when the military says "integrating," they're talking about, "You've got all these people on the same ship together." Okay, now what? So now that you've got 'em all together, you know, that should not count as integration, just because you've achieved that. Okay, okay it's an integration, but what kind of education do these people have? You know, [for example], "I'm a White guy from Iowa, you know. Only White, only Black people or any other people of color I've seen is on TV. And here I am, I'm put in the same department as this Black guy from New York. We may wind up killing each other." So what is the Navy doing to ... for understanding? I mean, really doing.

These points were prevalent throughout the study. Master Chief James agrees, and explains how the Navy's lack of effort in helping sailors understand cultural differences places the young African American sailor at a disadvantage:

I think the military has done a good job of integrating, you know, and having personnel of different cultures, different races. But where I think our problems lie is where we try to ... where we have issues because of the fact that we don't understand or we haven't dealt with the ... we don't know where these folks are coming from. Ah, take for example, if you have this young African American third class petty officer who gets offended when the individual, you know, curses at him, talks down to him, okay. Well, that Caucasian individual may feel, "Well, you know what? I talk to everyone that way. You know, and if I talk to everyone that way, you shouldn't be offended by it. Get over it." Well, he may keep doing it because he feels that he's not doing anything wrong because he does that to everyone. And that African American youth may let him know, "You know what, I don't like that. I don't take that. Don't do it." And then eventually, he'll be looked at as the bad guy because that same guy can say the same thing to, a young Caucasian, ah, sailor and that guy not get mad. So because the African American youth got mad, now he's the bad guy. So I think our biggest problem, our biggest, ah, gap is the understanding of cultures, you know.... When we were in boot camp it was that way because they had a hard time adapting, you know. Everyone wants discipline ... but the type of discipline that was being given was harder for that African American youth to take than maybe it was for the Caucasian individual. And maybe that was because they knew, that Caucasian knew that it was a game and knew not to take it personally, you know. They know at the end of it, everything was going to be alright and we can all go, you know, get some coffee and it'll all be over with and it'll be something that we can talk about. And that African American youth took it offensive, you know. When you told him, "Hey, you know what, you better do this or I'm gonna kick your ass," they took for granted, "You know what, this individual's gonna try to kick my ass." You know ... they're going and preparing themselves to make sure this don't happen. Whereas the Caucasian youth knows, "Hey this is just something somebody's saying just to be saying it." So, yea, all the diversity that we have and the big mix or the big ... the things that the Navy has done to make it better, there are still steps that we can take to make it more well-rounded ... to make it more of a success story for the African American youth. And the biggest part of that is understanding where he is coming from.

This lack of understanding — by both junior sailors and their supervisors — has serious consequences for efforts to create a meritocracy. As stated above, problems may arise between sailors due to a lack of cultural understanding. However, problems may also arise when supervisors fail to understand and sufficiently consider the cultural differences that may exist between them and those who work for them. Because these supervisors are the holders of power in these relationships, the junior African American sailor will likely be the one to suffer when conflict arises as a result of such lack of understanding.

Although they disagree that the military has created a meritocracy, most of those in the study believe the military has probably made more progress in this area than the greater American society. As Chief Butler aptly put it,

> My views on this is I wouldn't call it a success story, but I would say it's the most forward thinking, of a lot of our society. You've gotta keep in mind the military is nothing but a mix of society that's already out there in the world. So people already come in with their preconceived notions, whatever they may be. Because we are, one, directed to by instructions to give people those opportunities to happen. And secondly, there's a different respect level people have for one another once you are deployed. When you go out on a deployment and people see you got heart and you'll do whatever or what needs to be done to make a mission happen, you earn a different sort of respect that our civilian counterparts ... they're not privileged enough to see that. You know the type of pressure that that can put you under. People know what you're made of and once they find out what you're made of, then there's a different respect level. So in that way, the military is quite a bit [more] advanced than, you know, the civilian counterparts out there.

Another factor that distinguishes the military from civilian organizations is that the military expends significant resources to train its forces on issues relating to equal opportunity. Although, in many cases, they lack adequate measures of the effectiveness of the training programs, the military ensures all its personnel receive equal opportunity training at the point of entry and periodically thereafter. In comparing this effort to the efforts made in the civilian sector, Senior Chief Gregg asserts,

The military, they will continually try to train you. In the civilian sector, they'll say, "Okay, we're going to give you one sexual harassment class that's going to last." For example, "We're going to give one sexual harassment class and one diversity class when you first get hired." Now you may be with the company for 10 years and all you've had is that one class. That's it. But the one class is enough for them to say, "We told you." The military's training is a little more constant.

However, in spite of all the military's diversity training and efforts, divisions still exist. Thus, to claim that the services have created a meritocracy is to greatly exaggerate the progress they have made.

7

Resilience: How They Coped

> *Resilience. I had to be resilient.... And I can honestly say, what got me to where I am now was what I learned in the Navy.... And after the Navy, taking on obstacles and taking on challenges was, I wouldn't say a piece of cake, but easier for me to know how to deal with it. I was well-prepared. So in other words, when I ran into that proverbial brick wall, the brick wall would never stop me ... if I could, I would go around it. If I couldn't, I would go over it. If I had to, I dug under it and in some cases I went right through it. But the brick wall was never a permanent obstacle. I was always resilient.*
>
> — Senior Chief Evanston

The participants in this study identified many obstacles that they faced in their movement up through the military rank structure. Although each person had his own reasons for staying, the majority reported that at some point they had given consideration to quitting. A logical response to seemingly insurmountable barriers is reduced effort and sometimes a decision to altogether quit. This is especially true when those barriers appear to have been constructed for unjust reasons. However, few in this study considered quitting. As Chief Butler describes his own thoughts of quitting:

> Usually on deployment. Those were pretty much the only times. And it would be pretty much during really, really hard days ... you know, missing my kids and missing my family or something like that but that's all it was. It was just being homesick in the back of my mind, you know. You know, you being a former Chief, there's pretty much only one place you can really go and relax when you're out there, and that's in your rack. You know, those feelings I would get about ... maybe I want to find another career or something where I can be home or something like that. Those were really the only times it would come to me, was those nights when I was finally resting in my rack or some-

thing like that. But as a whole, I've never really thought about quitting. As a whole, I've enjoyed my job. I've really enjoyed being an ordnanceman. I enjoy the Navy, you know, for the most part. I think there are some things, you know, that have happened in recent years I have discomfort with, or I don't probably agree with, but as a whole I like the job.

Based on his comments, he seemed to believe that his thoughts of quitting were not caused by how he was treated in the Navy. When asked if his treatment by his peers ever caused him to think of quitting, he responded,

Oh no, not ever, because they don't feed my family. You know that ... I don't ... I don't put much, if any concern in that area at all. You know at the end of the day, they don't pay my paycheck. So I don't ... I'm not concerned with them not even a little bit.

Others discussed having to do things above and beyond what was normally required in order to be promoted. One constant theme among those in the study was the view that African American men had to do more in order to promote than did their White colleagues. As discussed by Master Chief Ivans,

I can tell you it was conflict and that was uncommon for me. I could see that I was succeeding, but the stress of it and the dilemmas ... at what expense? Like to achieve, I was what you could call a rate-grabber. I made E-1 to E-8 my first time up, so but people would say what do I have to complain about, I'm making rate. But I, I could see where others [who] were making rate wasn't doing what I was doing. Like, I did 3 straight tours at sea which was uncommon for my expertise and the program that I was in. I qualified Officer of the Deck underway. I was security manager, so forth. Items like that, that were far and beyond for my expertise ... and did get me promoted. But I knew if I didn't do these things, I saw others that were doing their jobs — ah, Black males — and not being promoted. So it was like, at ... the rewards were at what expense. And it was a constant dilemma with me to balance my personal life, my family and my, my Naval career. So I would look at it at times [and ask] is it worth it to what I'm trying to obtain. So it was always a period of, "Hey, just let this go and go ahead and do something else."

The feeling of having to do more than others in order to achieve the same status was clearly present among many of those in this study. Even those who were reluctant to say that race was a burden for them discussed the feeling of needing to do more than their White colleagues in order to attain the same level of achievement. While these men were willing to do more, the impact of *having* to do more clearly weighed on them.

In spite of these added burdens, the majority of those in the study did not retain hostilities toward the system once they achieved senior enlisted status. They disposed of these feelings in different ways. Some did this by framing their experiences in a way that highlights perceived benefits that they say they derived from having experienced the difficulties. As discussed by Senior Chief Evanston,

> This is the way I look at it. You take experience and you catalog it. You catalog it so that you always have that remembrance to go to, to help you with the situation that's happening in the present. That's what it's there for. You know, what I learned to do is when I would catalog it, I would catalog it through a filter and that filter was to remove any hate and negativity that would drag me down as a person. Because those people that hated me did not hate me because they knew me. They hated me because they were ignorant, because they were afraid, because they didn't understand. And when you keep that in that context, you just realize that all I have to do now is become more aware. So, I remember what happened to me in the Navy, but I'm not bitter because of it. I just took it as a lesson in life.

A few of the respondents did carry hostilities with them as they promoted to Chief and some hold to those hostilities today, including Master Chief Ivans:

> Yes, and I'd say it still lingers on today and like I said, I talked to my mentor, [who] retired as a Senior Chief, and I know he was definitely Master Chief Material.... But he was able to pass on some things to me that I was able to use and I've tried to pass on. But the negatives ... that I see even in my day-to-day dealings with the politics in the Navy, I've sat on awards boards, I've sat on disciplinary review boards and saw how it's personality driven ... and with personalities, I feel race, gender, and all that comes into play and most decisions are all made by White males. That, ah ... what's the word I'm looking for? How we equate the standards are totally different in that regard to ... especially on Black males. So that's been very difficult to deal with. I've been able to change some of that, as a Master Chief. But ... one alone is not going to be able to make a dent in how the Navy has passed this along with tradition through the years.

Though the majority did not hold on to hostilities and the others have managed to deal with those hostilities, each has found different ways to cope within this workplace where they feel they have not been fully accepted. The literature discusses many ways African Americans cope within predominantly White workplaces. Among these is minimizing expectations of achievement (Mirowsky and Ross, 1989), informal social and political networks (Cole and Omari, 2003), and withdrawal (Crocker and Major, 1989). The respondents in this study indicated some of these and other coping mechanisms.

Overachieving

Race is something that African American men cannot escape. A constant theme among those in the study was that they believed they either *had* to work and/or study harder, or that they *chose* to work and/or study harder. Chief Butler discussed a conversation that he had with his supervisor after having recently reported:

> I remember him telling me the type of things he would and would not tolerate ... all of those ... laziness and being to work on time and all that kinda thing ... and I remember ... taking offense to that because I'm like, "Wait, this guy don't know me from Adam" and after that moment, I made up in my mind that I'm gonna be the best worker here. I'm gonna be the best looking in my uniform, I'm gonna know the most, and I'm gonna be able to apply it better than anybody at this joint. I made it happen.

The feeling of having to do more than others in order to achieve the same status was clearly present among many of those in this study. Even those who were reluctant to say that race was a burden for them discussed the feeling of needing to do more than their White colleagues in order to attain the same level of achievement. While these men were willing to do more, the impact of *having* to do more clearly weighed on them, as Master Chief James explained:

> And maybe that's because I had to work harder. Or maybe I'm not saying I had to work harder. I chose to work harder than maybe they did to make sure I knew my job. Because they may have — and maybe some of this was preconceived on my part — I believe that I had to know more. I had to do more in order to make sure that I didn't fail.

Having to work harder for fewer rewards has the real potential to serve as a disincentive for continued effort. While these men clearly chose to keep trying, for some, having to work harder was de-motivating. Chief Ivans explained:

> It's common dialogue throughout my career with other African American, Black males that they feel that they work harder than, ah, the majority, particularly White males and they don't get the opportunities that some of them get, they're always told, "You can go next time" and next time don't seem to come and "This is what you need to work on." There were other ratings in this department as well at sea and it was common knowledge with them that they would see the same things. Ah, the attitude with them was "no matter how hard you work, ah others [who] was not working as hard as you, particularly White males is gonna get the rewards; gonna the awards ... get the, the schools ahead of you." So it was almost to the point where they felt as though you

were being used. You were being used as a worker bee and not being rewarded. So it was somewhat de-motivating for them. And I took the approach that I was gonna make it motivate me. I was gonna consistently request the schools, ah, ask questions on what I could do better and use that as self-improvement and look at what I could do. And also continue [to] communicate what I was seeing as I felt unfairly because I always did bring that up to my LPO and my Chief, in particular that incident that was current with me, that I felt as though I was a harder worker than the individual that came onboard the ship the same time I did, same rating, same time in grade and it seem as though he got the awards and the rewards going to school before I did.

Adaptation

Another coping mechanism disclosed in this study is the ability to strategize and adapt to overcome obstacles. The participants in this study were careful to differentiate between adapting for the purpose of fitting in and adapting to achieve their objectives. They clearly rejected any notion that they changed their tastes, class of friends, or any other personal aspect of their lives in order to be accepted by the Navy's White majority. However, they did discuss adjusting tactics for the purpose of overcoming barriers. Discussing the need to wear a "mask," Chief Hines stated:

> What I have learned a long time ago is that I have to be or possess the ability to be able to adapt to my environment whatever the environment is. I think it was Langston Hughes or Paul Lawrence Dunbar that talked about "We wear the mask." Sometimes I have felt like I had to put on a glass face and other times I was very genuine about the interactions I had in order to allow myself to be heard because there were many times I was speaking and I know that people were pretty much ignoring me. Even though what I had to say was relevant and pertinent to what was being discussed and was probably the solution that largely went ignored. So I developed methods for making myself be heard by attaching my comments to others who I knew was respected. I might attribute part of what I was saying to them in order to make it be heard and accepted.

Frequently, the participants in the study discussed their methods by which they achieved their objectives. Chief Butler provided one example:

> Let's take in a board like we're doing input to a sailor of the quarter, sailor of the year, or any award, something like that.... When I have to speak for somebody, I have to be dramatic, it has to have full impact for anybody to, to give any credit or validation to what I'm saying. I can't simply come into a room and say, "This guy is doing well because he did this. Therefore I nominate him." If I did that, a lot of the people I represent would get jack. And I've seen it done. I've really seen it done. So, when it's time for those things, I

really have to do homework and I have to practice what I'm gonna say to the rest of my brothers in the Chiefs' mess for impact. I have to be dramatic about it for them to get their fair shake.

Adaptation to the circumstances was mentioned frequently in the discussion with the participants. Some of the strategies used were more dramatic than others. Senior Chief Gregg discussed how he adapted his behavior to overcome performance restrictions that were being placed on him by a senior naval officer:

[A]ctually the hardest time I had was when I actually made Chief. Once I actually put the Chief's uniform on that's when I ran into all craziness. Especially on the ship. When the, ah, Chief who was there, he was getting ready to leave and the commander that he worked for—I can't straight up say he didn't like Blacks because ... but I can straight up say he didn't like women—so to me I could say, if you were a minority, he didn't like you.... You know, this wasn't my first ship, so I knew what I had to do. But he was just, "Don't do it." So anytime, you know some serious situation came up, he just tried to bowl me over, "We're going to do it this way." I'm like, "Commander, the book says we have to do it this way; we're gonna do it this way." You know, he'd say, "Are you arguing with me?" [I'd say] "No sir, I'm not arguing with you. We'll do it your way."

Recognizing that the Commander—a senior commissioned officer—had usurped his responsibilities as the senior technician, Senior Chief Gregg adapted his tactics to the situation:

Now, you've got 20 airplanes in the air, no radar and it's dark outside. And my boss, she's sitting right behind me as I'm doing this and she's saying ... and she's talking to the commander on the phone and the commander is telling her to "do this, and do this, and do this." And she looked at me and said, "Chief, the commander said do this, do this, do this." I said, "We're not going to do that. This is what we're going to do." And she's kinda like freaked out. She got ulcers from him. She goes, "I don't think I can tell him that." I said, "Well, you need to tell him that." And then she told him. Soon as she told him that, he comes'—'cause he's right next door—he comes busting through the door and you've got a room full of E-3s up to E-5s and E-6s all in there right there, 20 of 'em in the room and he comes running right up to my face blathering at the mouth, "You will do what I tell you and you will do this, this, this and this and you...." I said, "Commander, what you want to do is not safe and is illegal. I know exactly what this book says; I know exactly what I'm doing.... What I'm going to do is this, this, this, this, this, this. I recommend that you call the captain and let him know that this is what the deal is." And he just looked at me. And he turned around and walked away.... From that point on, he left me alone. He never said anything to me; he just concentrated his efforts on the women. You know, just being negative toward them. But he left me alone. From that point on, he was like ... we were cool. You know, he could joke with me now. Before, he wouldn't.

This Chief adapted his strategy to one of confrontation and stood up to the senior officer who he perceived to have been unjustly denying him his autonomy. However, he did this based on his proficiency in what he was doing. Senior Chief Evanston, in discussing how he used confrontation, made it clear that there is a right way and a wrong way to use this strategy:

> But one thing that I always caution myself on is ... the timing of it and how I went about doing it, because another thing that I ... was communicated to me by a Petty Officer — because at the time I was a seaman — is I could be labeled as a troublemaker or as a person that brings problems to the chain of command and that would be looked on as [un]favorable for me.

Through discussing his own experiences, Chief Hines provided an example of how failure to appropriately adapt can affect impact one's careers:

> I've always been outspoken. What I mean is if I have an opportunity to address something, it didn't have to be contradictory, adversarial, or any of that. If I saw it, I was going to speak on it if I felt it needed to be addressed. I would get comments on my evaluations from my White superiors that would say as such: "tends to be a little outspoken." I'm not quite sure what that was supposed to mean other than the fact that "he speaks about things he should keep to himself." Of course the things I spoke about were true and everyone saw it and everyone knew it.

While adaptation and overachieving served as outward actions that helped these men cope with their circumstances while continuing to ascend the military rank structure, they also employed internal coping mechanisms that prevented the obstacles from leading to despondence. Perhaps more than the outward reactions, it is the internal coping mechanisms that facilitate perseverance.

Minimization

Ruggiero, et al. (1997) suggest that individuals avoid stress by denying the presence of discrimination even when significant evidence of such discrimination exists. This, they say, reduces the stress associated with the vulnerability caused by the loss of the sense of control resulting from discrimination. Several of the participants in this study demonstrated a different type of minimization, whereby they acknowledged the existing barriers, but minimized their importance. By minimizing the importance of these barriers, the participants were able to avoid despondence and continue to work to overcome the unjust obstacles they saw in front of them. In demonstrating this, Chief Carter discussed the barriers that were erected to prevent him from being promoted:

> I don't think race had much to do with me being promoted. I think it was the individual's own perception that held me from being promoted. It wasn't ... I don't know what was going through ... maybe it was race. Maybe not. It probably had something to do with it.

Chief Carter, in discussing the significance of personal associations, sought to minimize the importance of race and illuminate the significance of favoritism based on other factors:

> Well, you got your supervisors there, and you know, that regardless of what you know and what you do, if this individual has some type of bad feeling toward you for whatever reason, [for example] he feels you should be doing something else. When it comes down to evaluation time, you, you know regardless of what your job is, how many people you got working for you, it's always the, ah, close-to-the-throne syndrome. What I mean by that is that individual could be a slacker or whomever, if he's close to the individual that's doing the write-up, well it's obvious that that individual's gonna get a better write-up, regardless of what type of work'" you're doing at the time.

As suggested by Mirowsky and Ross (1989), one's minority status tends to be associated with a reduced sense of control. Since he has no control over his minority status, one way the African American male service member may cope with the accompanying stress is to subordinate the importance of his minority status to other more controllable factors. This reduces the likelihood of despondence and enables him to continue to work toward success. When discussing why he was not included in many social functions held by his White colleagues, Chief Butler was careful to identify other causes for the exclusion. As he explained it,

> I would probably say ... I don't know. It could have been the way I looked, the way I dressed. Because you know I still dress like, like I would normally dress when I'm back home. I wear jeans, I wear t-shirts. I mean they wear jeans and t-shirts but different styles. Different styles, you know, there's ... there's ... everybody's got their own styles, whatever that may be, and I think my style was not a fit with their style. You know they were going to hang out at a bar and listen to some country music whereas I can do some country music for a little bit but I don't intend to do that my whole ... all the time that I have liberty.

However, when asked if it was possible that he was trying to avoid the topic of race, he quickly responded:

> I probably am. But I think there are some racial ... there were some racial things involved with it as well. Since I've been a Chief, everywhere I've been, I've been the only Black khaki there. Everywhere I've been. And that...it sometimes, you know, it may be me ... I don't know. Or it may be the rest of my peer group. But I have expectations as well. You know, I, when I walk in the door somewhere I give the benefit of the doubt to everybody there. You know I think that people are people regardless of who they are, where they come from, religious background or any of that..... Sometimes I ... I wonder if people think that, that I have got some sort of different agenda. You know, because I don't. I think I'm the average American who happens to who happens to have ... people have a different opinion after they see me or hear my name or something like that. You know how the Chief community is. People know well before you do who you are if you're coming to their command. They've already talked to somebody who knows you or knows of you or something like that. And if they don't recognize the name they'll, they'll find out. You know, they'll find out what kind of guy you are and what kind of work you do. And my name is pretty ... it's kinda easy to realize that I'm probably not Caucasian if you see my name ... come up on orders.

The participants in the study clearly indicated the importance of not allowing race to be an acceptable cause of not succeeding. Master Chief James offered some sage advice to young African American sailors:

> I'd say, "First of all, you have to remember that you can be and you can do whatever you wanna do." You know, the only limits that you actually have are the limits that you put on yourself. [B]ut you sit there and listen to society or listen, sometimes ... even to that friend, you will for some reason believe that you can't do something or that you're hindered from doing something, and it may not be true. You may tend to be your own hindrance. The system has a lot of things out there available to you. For a lot, for some reasons, we, as African Americans, may not grab it as quickly as that Caucasian. Maybe it's because we don't have it instilled in us that you're what it's there for. You should go for it. It's there for you like it is for everybody else. And maybe that comes from the fact that we don't see a lot of African Americans in the senior leadership positions. So you feel because you don't see 'em there, then maybe that's not for me. Maybe it's not meant for me to be there. But you've gotta think around that, you know.

Self-Definition

In spite of all of the obstacles they faced, the participants in this study refused to allow others to define who they were. Although several stated that their competence was often questioned, none of those in the study stated a belief that their performance or competence was less than that of their White colleagues. Rather, they drew clear distinctions between how they defined themselves and how they were perceived by those who they say treated them unjustly. Each considered himself to be at least as competent as his White colleagues. When asked about his competence, Chief Andrews explains,

> I have no doubt that I'm just as competent as the person standing next to me. They might not think so. I don't think I'm incompetent or [that I] can't measure up to someone because they happen to be a White male or anything like that.

Although he expressed confidence in his own competence, when asked if his supervisors and others considered him as competent, he stated,

> Probably not, because I'm a young Black male. I sometimes believe there are those that are particularly in a leadership or management position that second guess or don't be taking me seriously. I think it's a combination of my race and age.

Mirowsky and Ross (1989) suggest that some African Americans, believing they will never fit in and be accepted, come to accept that Whites will always have the advantage and minimize expectations for their own achievement. However, this phenomenon was not evidenced among the men in this study. Although some chose to minimize the importance of the discrimination they faced, none minimized his expectation for success. Instead, they worked harder to succeed in spite of what they perceived to have been injustices. Moreover, because many believed they had to perform at a higher level, some considered themselves more competent than their White colleagues. These expressions of confidence were a constant theme among the participants in the study. Senior Chief Evanston asserted,

> See, the one thing that really got me through a lot was because I was so damn good at my field. I mean, it became ... in some cases I was very cocky about the fact that I was so good at what I did. And I exuded confidence. When it came to my field, I always felt I was second to no one. That was, I believe, one of my edges. So no matter how much anybody disliked me or no matter what kind of crap I went through, in very few situations did anybody challenge my expertise in what I did. I studied my butt off. I always did my research. I always made a point that when I opened my mouth, I knew what the hell I was talking about and that I was right.

Rewards in the form of medals and ribbons are two of the ways the Navy shows appreciation for a sailor's competence and superior performance. Similarly, a failure to receive these medals and ribbons is an indicator that the sailor's performance is not above average. Many of the men in this study indicated that they do not believe they received the rewards they deserved. However, they sought other means of deriving appreciation for their performance, which they believed to be superior. Chief Butler explained this in his discussion of his own experiences. Discussing whether he believed he was appropriately rewarded, he stated,

> Do I think it's at the level it should be? No. But I have [been rewarded] you know. Since I've become a Chief I've had three Navy Achievements. I think I've ... some of the things I think I've done I should have been accommodated for you know, a Navy Comm, you know. As well as being the ordnance Chief in the command, I was the first guy to accept the brand new mod of airplane. Some of the other people that were in that same command, they were showing me the coin that the skipper gave them. You know, to say that they developed the first ICAP III aircraft and accepted the first ICAP III aircraft and I'm like, wow, I was the sole maintenance controller, with no others, and the skipper didn't give me one of those coins. He didn't even give me an end of tour award. When it was time to go, he just let me go. And I've been awarded but my rewards don't come really in medals and paper because not everybody's going to pat you on the back. My rewards come in seeing those people I was mentioning earlier be successful to get past whatever stereotype might be out there because in my experience in the Navy, there's one thing that speaks for you louder than anything else, that's work performance. If you can prove to people that you're the top notch as far as work goes, they tend to stop forgetting what you look like because they know what you do.

These men defined themselves and the definition was one that recognized their competence as equal to, or greater than, that of their White colleagues. Further, in spite of the barriers they believe they had to overcome, the majority believed that their service in the Navy has made a difference. When asked about having made a difference, Senior Chief Gregg discussed the impact he believes he had on the lives of young African Americans:

> I made a difference in the lives of a lot of young Black people. Especially once I made Chief and Senior Chief, I was somebody that — especially in the air traffic control world — I was somebody that a Black E-3 can go, "Wow, it can be done." And I would help them as long as they helped themselves. I would help them. You know, that means a lot to them to see that. They'd say, "How did you get to where you are?" [I'd say], "this is how I got to where I am. This is what you need to do." And like the Master Chief who mentored me when I was an E-3, I turned it around and did that for others. And it made me feel good to see them move up the ranks.

Although he stated he made a difference in the lives of young Black sailors, when asked if he believes he made any real long term difference, Senior Chief Gregg responded:

> No. On an individual basis, maybe. Because a lot of those folks, I don't know where they are. But I think in the long-term, I think not. You know, I know I didn't change the minds of any White males ... I confronted a lot of the White males, and just issues of "I'm not doing that just because you say it. I don't care about that." You know, or try to teach them or show them that "your way is not the only way. You know, your way is just a way. Here goes some options, no matter what it is." But I knew if the majority agree with it, it would happen. They weren't happy. The only thing that would make them happy is when I left. You know, the main thing about me is I'm not going to do anything just because you said so. I'm definitely not going to do anything because you're the majority.

While Senior Chief Gregg believed he affected the lives of some young African American sailors, he clearly believes that systemic changes are needed and he was unable to effect the necessary long-term change. Chief Hines, however, expressed a view that was more typical of the participants in the study. He was happy to have made a difference in the lives of some sailors, even if the system has not been changed. Referring to an analogy of a boy saving a single starfish, he stated, "It made a difference to that one." Other participants pointed to an impact they had on the specific organization in which they were assigned. Senior Chief Ivans' response typified this:

> I can say when I was on a minesweeper in Ingleside, when I came onboard the ship, it's very important for the Chiefs to work together. It appeared to me that the Chief's mess was somewhat divided. Only certain Chiefs could speak up, and so it went through the whole command like that. I was the first Black male Chief to come on that ship ah in some time. And it really set a tone for some of the Black male sailors that, that they ... I guess they had a role model to look up to. And it was somewhat disturbing in the Chiefs' mess at first because at first it was a challenge for them, on how they were gonna deal with me. I learned that by communicating within the mess, communicating with the XO and the captain, the views that I had, ah, communicating the concerns [of] not only the Black sailors, but all sailors, and being listened to and seeing that implemented and have the Chiefs' mess rally and come together. I think that was a big accomplishment because it could have really definitely went in the other, opposite direction and the Chiefs' mess could have become divided more, but we pulled together and they started to ... because some of the White males, specifically the enginemen on that ship, I ... in my observation I considered them what I call a typical red-neck, each was on his own agendas all the time and anybody who spoke something different than what he wanted to do was always against him and he was gonna try to get rid of him. So within my first 2 weeks on board, he tried to get rid of two Black males. And when we brought 'em in for disciplinary review board I pointed out to him that this was not uncommon. And what was he doing to mentor and to help develop

him? And at first, me and him were really at odds but we came to develop a relationship, that I was not trying to tell him how to do his job. We were just trying to do business as a Chiefs' mess and other Chiefs seen that and they seen me standing up for what I thought was right, helping to pull the Chiefs' mess together and also pull that command closer together. So I think that's one of my top accomplishments.

8

Profiles in Struggle and Service

> *What I have learned a long time ago is that I have to be or possess the ability to be able to adapt to my environment whatever the environment is. I think it was Langston Hughes or Paul Lawrence Dunbar that talked about "We wear the mask." Sometimes I have felt like I had to put on a glass face and other times I was very genuine about the interactions I had in order to allow myself to be heard because there were many times I was speaking and I know that people were pretty much ignoring me. Even though what I had to say was relevant and pertinent to what was being discussed and was probably the solution that largely went ignored. So I developed methods for making myself be heard by attaching my comments to others who I knew was respected. I might attribute part of what I was saying to them in order to make it be heard and accepted.*
> — Chief Hines

The military boldly claims that it has created a meritocracy within a society where inequality seems to permeate so many aspects of life. However, the literature shows that African American men within the Navy are more likely to receive negative discharges, are less likely to promote to the most senior officer and enlisted ranks, are more likely to be subjected to the judicial and non-judicial punishment system, and are disproportionately represented among those on the military's death row. These statistics bear a striking resemblance to those of the greater American society. In spite of the statistics, however, the services boldly proclaim that they, above all others, have created a society — within the larger society — where merit alone determines one's level of achievement. Further, such claims are largely advanced by those who, as a group, have never existed within a marginalized group within the United States.

However, senior enlisted African American men, who exist within the system, offer a much different view of the service to which they have devoted much of their lives. This research shows that African American men believe that many barriers to full inclusion remain and that the achievement levels that they have attained have been reached in spite of those barriers.

Competence Questioned

Even in 2006, African American men in the U.S. Navy find their competence questioned by seniors and peers alike. Such questioning may have significant ramifications for their careers and the careers of those sailors over whom they exercise authority. Moreover, they assert that similar scrutiny is not applied to their White male colleagues of equal rank. The military requires that their technical experts and enlisted managers be competent, and a lack of faith in such competence will likely affect the autonomy that is granted and the type of work that is assigned. Indeed, several of the men in this study discussed scenarios where either they were not allowed to perform their functions with the requisite and typical autonomy or where they were not assigned to positions commensurate with their level of expertise and seniority. In the Navy, this can have a major impact on the careers of sailors. The types of jobs assigned and level of autonomy exercised greatly impact a sailor's performance evaluation. Such evaluations, combined with other factors, determine who is selected for promotions. These evaluations are particularly important for promotions to the senior enlisted ranks, where there are no examinations and promotions are determined based on the totality of a sailor's career as depicted in his performance evaluations.

Additionally, when these African American men's competence is questioned, the impact may be felt by those junior sailors who report to them. Many decisions that are made regarding the careers of junior enlisted sailors are made based on the recommendations of those sailors' supervisors. When those supervisors are not considered equally competent to their peers, it may be more difficult for them to effectively advocate for awards and other forms of recognition for their junior sailors. As a result, those junior sailors may be unjustly denied important recognition that may impact their promotion opportunities. Several of the Chiefs in this study presented scenarios where they advocated for recognition for African American men who report to them and found the credibility of such recommendations questioned. In the Navy — where Chiefs are typically considered the technical experts and seasoned senior enlisted managers — the questioning of credibility on recommendations is out of the ordinary. Furthermore, since it is the Chiefs who assign tasks and monitor the performance of these junior sailors, surely they would be the ones who would know more about the quality of these sailors' work performance. However, if the Chiefs themselves are not believed to be competent, their evaluation of the sailors who report to them is likely to be questioned.

Though it may or may not be apparent to those in positions of leadership, the failure to receive due recognition may have implications far beyond the particular recognition in question and impact overall morale and discipline, placing the sailors in a downward spiral. If sailors are repeatedly denied recognition they believe they have earned, they may eventually reduce their level of performance, further reducing the probability of promotion. Additionally, tensions that may arise from the feeling of being unjustly treated may cause these junior sailors to act out in ways that violate the Uniform Code of Military Justice. Again, this further damages the sailors' careers by reducing promotion opportunities or it may, in fact, lead to demotion.

In-Group/Out-Group

Another barrier identified in this study is the presence of a network where those who are a part of an "in-group" receive preferential treatment. The participants identified this network as a group of primarily White males who work to advance the careers of junior White sailors. Because there are a finite number of positions available in each rank, when preference is given to some sailors, other sailors — those who are in the "out-group"— are necessarily disadvantaged. Because of the design of the Navy's advancement system, there are numerous ways some sailors could be advantaged while others are placed at a disadvantage. Those in this study identified position assignments as one way White sailors' careers are advanced through favoritism. For example, by placing these junior sailors in supervisory positions, senior members of the "good ol' boys' network" positioned them for increased visibility and opportunities to excel. Participants discussed situations where they believe junior sailors were selected, because of their race, to be in positions of leadership over them. Chiefs are typically allowed full authority to decide how their personnel are assigned, and when such assignments are done based on favoritism, those who are not members of the "in-group" are placed at a disadvantage.

How decisions are made about who receives specialized training is another way participants in this study say African American males are sometimes placed at a disadvantage. Such specialized training prepares these sailors for positions of increased authority and responsibility and may also help prepare them to do well on promotion examinations. Additionally, the increased authority and responsibility that may result from this training may be reflected positively in the sailors' performance evaluations, further adding to the advantage. Some participants discussed scenarios where they believe decisions about who was sent to specialized schools were made based on favoritism. Others discussed situations where Chiefs provided training opportunities on the ship exclusively for White male sailors. In either case, the extra training provides some with an added advantage that better equips them to compete for the limited number of positions at the next higher rank.

Another important factor is the belief that the Navy engages in a form of "reverse discrimination," where African American men and other historically marginalized groups receive institutionalized preference in promotions. Although this view is false, some in this study expressed the belief that, because they are African American, the Navy grants them preference. A similar belief exists among some White sailors. The result of this is White sailors questioning whether African American men are competent and whether they actually earned their rank.

Some participants in this study stated that, until they were promoted to Master Chief and had actually participated as a member of the selection boards, they had believed that preference was being granted to African Americans and other minority groups based on their race. They added that once they realized this was not true, they were pleased to know that they were not promoted because of their race. However, the majority of sailors never serve on promotion boards and many continue to hold to the belief that African Americans are promoted, not based on their merit, but because of their race. As a result, many continue to question African American men's competence and to blame their own failure to promote on "reverse discrimination." Such beliefs serve as a barrier to full inclusion.

Limited Role Models

Another barrier is the limited number of senior enlisted African American males who serve as role models. This study revealed how some African American men are affected by not seeing African American male role models in senior leadership positions. When there are no African Americans to show that it is possible for them to ascend to the most senior levels, it may be difficult for some young African American males to see how they can rise to those levels. Some segments of the Navy — particularly some aviation and submarine specialties — have very few African Americans and even fewer in positions of leadership. Moreover, in its more than 225 years of existence, the Navy has never had an African American serve as the Master Chief Petty Officer of the Navy — the most senior enlisted position in the Navy. This is particularly revealing, considering the fact that this person is appointed to this position by the Chief of Naval Operations, the most senior officer position, which is also an appointed position that has never been filled by an African American.

The importance of role models may not be fully appreciated by those who have historically made, and who continue to make, the overall decisions in the Navy. White men in the United States have never been lacking in role models because they have always been the ones making the rules. Similarly, the Navy provides White men with ample role models — at all levels of leadership — who bear their skin color. However, for African American men and other historically marginalized groups, role models are a source of hope and optimism that they too can achieve the higher levels of leadership. Moreover, only those in higher level positions can truly provide the most effective mentorship for juniors aspiring to reach the highest levels, because only they have learned by experience what it takes to attain those levels of leadership.

While those in positions of leadership — predominantly White men — assert that the military has managed to create an institution where race does not matter when it comes to achievement, African American men — those who have been historically marginalized — disagree. Moreover, I am aware of no empirical evidence that supports such a sweeping assertion. The Navy makes these assertions in spite of its own statistics, which show a significant gap in all measures of achievement between African American men and their White colleagues. Whether it is in advancement rates or discipline statistics, types of discharges or incarceration rates, African American men fare far worse than do their White male counterparts.

The military's claims are not without consequences. If the military has created this meritocracy, then there would be no need to continue efforts to eradicate inequality. Although, over the years, the military services have led society in taking proactive measures to eliminate discrimination based on race from their ranks, the services' commitment to this effort seems to have waned. In the 1980s, the Department of Defense established the Defense Race Relations Institute (which later became the Defense Equal Opportunity Management Institute (DEOMI)), where representatives from all services underwent 16 weeks of in-depth training on various aspects of inequality in order to assist commanders in creating more just working environments. However, in recent years, that training has been reduced by over 37 percent. Additionally, Navy commanders were required to issue personal statements to their organizations, declaring their commitment to equal opportunity and requiring that all others support the Navy's equal opportunity policy. In recent years, however, that requirement has been eliminated and many commanders no longer issue such statements. Further, where the Navy once required its organizations to annually assess their equal opportunity climates using reliable and valid methods, they now may use any method those organizations choose, even those that are likely to be unreliable and invalid.

Moreover, the military's assertions of meritocracy may lead to complacency or they may serve as cover for those who wish to maintain the status quo. This could have a significant impact on military readiness. In a time when some of the military services struggle to meet recruitment goals and to retain personnel, the status quo may not be sufficient to retain qualified African American men. Although those in this study stayed to reach the most senior enlisted ranks, it is not at all clear that the services are not presently losing personnel at the lower levels due to perceptions of inequality and feelings that there is a lack of opportunity.

But They Coped

Military personnel often enter the military with no intention of staying. The same is true of those in this study. The participants stated several different reasons for enlisting and staying in the military. Some say they enlisted because of relatives who had previously served, while others say they enlisted to change their life's circumstances. However, few of the participants say they had initially planned to stay for an entire career.

Again, each had his own reason for staying. The majority say they stayed in order to provide financial support for their family.

Whatever their reasons were for enlisting and for staying, each identified methods of coping in the face of what he considered inequality. As in other sectors of American life, the African American men in this study stated that they believed it was necessary for them to work and study harder than did their White colleagues. None stated that this requirement was imposed on him by his supervisors. However, because of their perceptions of existing preconceived notions that African American men are less hard-working and are less intelligent, many feel as if they begin at a deficit and must work harder in order to overcome these stereotypes and demonstrate that they are just as hard-working and that they are as intelligent as their White male colleagues. While White sailors are judged as individuals, many African American male sailors — as well as many African Americans in society at large — believe that they are often judged as a group and that their abilities are judged based on how their group is perceived.

Another method that is used to cope with perceived inequality is to minimize the impact such inequality has on one's life chances. Each participant in this study discussed the existence of barriers to full inclusion for African American men. However, several seemed to downplay the impact these barriers have had on their own careers. Yet, those who did seem to downplay the impact of these barriers on their careers clearly articulated how such barriers were affecting the careers of those sailors who worked for them. Mirowsky and Ross (1989) suggest that minority status is associated with less control because, for minorities, "any given level of achievement requires greater effort and provide fewer opportunities" (p. 16). One result, they suggest, is that rather than enduring the stress caused by this, many minorities will lower their expectations. However, another result may be that, rather than lower their expectations for achievement or deny the existence of inequality, they deny the significance of the inequality on *their* own careers. Yet, once the analysis changes and they are considering the impact the inequality has on the careers of *others*, they can more clearly see how others are disadvantaged. Such coping mechanism allows these men to maintain a sense of control over their own destiny without denying the existence of inequalities.

Although minimization serves as an important coping mechanism by preventing despondence and allowing these men to continue to strive to achieve, it may also delay the necessary confrontation that is required to forge change. By not acknowledging the true impact inequalities have on *their* careers, they likely reduce the probability that they will point out these inequalities and oppose the status quo. Moreover, if future generations of sailors adopt a similar coping strategy, real change may be very slow in coming. It is necessary for those who are disadvantaged to challenge the system and inform those who are privileged. Otherwise, having never been a part of an "out-group," those in the majority may never truly understand.

Several participants in the study discussed how they adapted in order to cope with the barriers they faced in different Navy organizations. Sometimes this adaptation involved changing from a more passive posture to a more confrontational one. Other times it involved strategizing on how best to confront selection boards in order to achieve the desired outcomes. In either case, these men gave considerable thought to the course of action they would take prior to acting. Although adaptation is often necessary when confronting many different challenges, and this is not unique to African American men, adapting to overcome the effects of racial inequality is different because it is an added burden that only members of marginalized groups must bear. Further, there are psychological costs associated with having to adapt to overcome burdens that exist due to one's race or other non-merit factor. Those in the study expressed frustration when discussing the need to work to overcome the impact their race has on their career opportunities and those of their subordinate sailors.

However, in spite of the added burdens they believe existed because of their race, each indicated that he was not defined by others, but that he knew and had confidence in himself. This point was a major theme throughout the study. While some stated that they felt pressures to change in order to "fit in" with their White peers, none stated he submitted to those pressures. Moreover, some stated that fitting in was not a concern for them. Just as minimizing the impact of discrimination helped these men to continue to strive to achieve, their refusal to see themselves as they were represented by some of their supervisors also helped them to be persistent in working toward their goals. In each case—whether it was when their supervisors and peers questioned their competence, attempted to minimize their autonomy, failed to give them the assignments they felt they had earned, or failed to give them the awards they felt they had earned—these men chose to define themselves. Moreover, they defined themselves in a way that showed them as equal to, or more competent than, their peers.

Further, while Feagin and Sikes (1994) discussed organizations engaging in social cloning to groom upwardly mobile employees to act in ways that are comfortable for the majority, the participants in this study did not seem very concerned about this. Although some did say that there were certain topics of discussion that they would avoid in the presence of their White colleagues, the majority rejected the notion that they altered their behaviors or conversations in order to avoid offending their White colleagues. Further, by defining themselves, rather than submitting to the view presented by some of their supervisors and colleagues, the participants avoided submitting to the view that their minority status afforded them less control over their careers as discussed by Mirowsky and Ross (1989). Instead, they worked and studied harder and achieved in spite of the obstacles they perceived existed due to their minority status.

Negative Feelings

In spite of the obstacles they say they faced, the majority of those in the study say they did not retain any negative feelings about their experiences once they were selected for Chief. Some stated that they just accepted that they would face racists and that they refused to be bitter about their experiences. Others saw it as a victory for themselves in spite of efforts by some to prevent them from succeeding. One participant summed it up by stating, "What I felt was that even though I had to work harder, I still felt that I out-bested the process. So for me, that was a personal victory. That, in itself, was worth celebrating and saying, 'See, I knew I could do it.' I wasn't going to carry anything else as weight."

Although the majority of participants stated they retained no negative feelings, a significant minority did hold on to negative feelings resulting from their experiences as they came up through the ranks. Events that happen in one's past often affect one's level of attainment in the present or the future. One participant stated that he still holds on to hostilities because, had he been fairly treated earlier in his career, he would likely have attained a higher rank. This raises a question within the Navy context with which the greater American society continues to grapple: How can we get to a purely merit-based system and call it equal when people begin at different places as a result of past inequalities? This is a question that the Navy must consider as it works to create a more just and equal workplace.

9

Implications for Navy Policies: A Prescription for Change

As many in this research suggest, the military — perhaps more than other organizations — has devoted significant resources to eradicating inequalities from its ranks. The services have created policies prohibiting discrimination and have provided its members means of seeking redress when they feel their rights have been violated. Additionally, they invest large sums of money each year in training programs designed to prevent incidents of discrimination. The establishment of the Defense Equal Opportunity Management Institute — a training institute that is dedicated to educating service members on issues relating to inequalities and providing strategies for change — demonstrated a significant commitment to creating a more equal working environment.

However, in spite of its efforts, the evidence suggests that the military still has not created an environment where merit alone determines one's level of attainment. Sailors still point to situations where they believe career decisions are made based on factors other than merit. Further, they contend that White men — regardless of competence — often receive advantages in awards, assignments, evaluations, training, mentorship, promotions, and other areas that are major determinants of one's level of attainment within the Navy. Moreover, statistics show that the outcomes of such inequalities are similar to those in society at large, leaving African American men less likely to attain the most senior enlisted and officer ranks, more likely to be subjected to the military's judicial and non-judicial punishment systems, and more likely to receive a punitive discharge.

Reassess the Current State

If the Navy is to continue to progress and move toward its goal of a more egalitarian workplace, where race or cultural background is not a factor in determining one's level of success, it must take concrete steps to create change. First, the service must begin to view meritocracy as an aspiration rather than reality. In asserting that the goal has been attained, the service implies that injustice has been eradicated and that there is no work left to do in this area. The consequences of this are quite significant and are currently being revealed in the Navy's actions and policies. For example, where unit commanders were previously required to issue personal statements declaring their commitment to equal opportunity and requiring that all others under his or her charge demonstrate a similar commitment, current Navy policy contains no such requirement. This personal policy statement, when thoughtfully written, served as a powerful indicator to those throughout the command of the commander's views on this issue. Moreover, it impressed upon employees the commander's expectations of them.

Just as the presence of these statements makes powerful statements, the absence of them makes an equally powerful statement. Although some commanders continue to issue written policy statements in spite of the fact that there is no regulation mandating them, many feel that such policies are no longer required and do not issue them. This is a reasonable response to the assertion that meritocracy has been achieved. However, for those service members of all races and backgrounds who are accustomed to seeing such statements, this may signal a retreat from the efforts to create a more equal working environment. Moreover, it may signal to many in positions of authority that they are free to influence careers as they choose. Many will choose to do so without consideration for merit. For members of traditionally marginalized groups, it could signal a lack of concern for their professional well-being.

Another consequence of the assertion of meritocracy is being reflected in the military's funding for equal opportunity training. The training, which previously lasted 16 weeks, has been reduced to 10 weeks. In reducing the length of the course, components of the training that were critical to helping participants gain a better understanding of the dynamics of privilege in society and in the military have been removed or scaled back. Further, while reducing the course length by 37 percent provides additional time to increase the number of classes taught, the services actually reduced the number of classes taught each year. Such drastic reductions send a clear signal that the military has begun to retreat on its efforts to create a more equal workplace.

Eliminating the requirement to use valid and reliable instruments to test Navy organizations' equal opportunity climates is another fall-out from the assertion that a meritocracy has been achieved. Organizational climate assessments served as valuable tools which allowed personnel at all levels an opportunity to articulate their honest views of the organization's equal opportunity climate. Previously, the Navy provided each organization the freedom to use specific instruments — such as the Military Equal Opportunity Climate Survey (MEOCS) and Command Assessment Team System Survey (CATSYS) — that were determined to be reliable and valid for examining their organizational climates. These instruments were designed to be combined with additional interviews, observations, and a review of records and reports. However, in recent years, the Navy has eliminated all specific guidance to organizations on how to evaluate their equal opportunity climates. The current requirement is that commanders test their climates each year and that they use any methods they choose — including large group discussions that are facilitated by the commander. The use of such methods is not likely to yield accurate results because junior personnel are not likely to express their honest views in large groups that provide no anonymity or safeguards against reprisals. Moreover, because of the large difference in rank between the commanding officer and junior officers and enlisted personnel, these large group discussions are not likely to provide a true portrait of the organization's equal opportunity climate. Instead, they usually result in one-way conversations, with the commanding officer talking to the junior personnel while they sit quietly.

The military's assertion of meritocracy is doing significant damage to the services' aspiration of creating a more equal workplace. In addition to impacting the amount of resources and effort that are being devoted to this cause, the assertion also has the potential to add to the negative perception of African American men. If, in spite of the existence of a meritocracy, African American men remain less likely to promote to the senior ranks, and more likely to receive punishment, what does that say about these men? A reasonable conclusion would be that they are less intelligent, less hard working, and more crime-prone. The result of such analysis is that many White men will continue to hold to faulty views of superiority.

Leadership Top-Down: Create an Equal Opportunity Climate

In the Navy, as in other organizations, the top leadership sets the climate. However, unlike many other organizations, Navy commanding officers exercise enormous control over those under their command. Penalties for disobeying a commanding officer's orders go far beyond impact on promotions and could range from stiff fines and restrictions on movement to jail time. If the Navy is ever to achieve its professed goal of a purely merit-based organization, commanders must make this effort one of their top priorities. Others throughout the organization set their priorities based on the commander's priorities. Similarly, when commanders lack interest in a goal, so do those under their command.

There are many steps commanders can take to demonstrate their commitment to equal opportunity. One way is to publish a clear policy statement, ensuring such policy is disseminated to those in the organization so that they may clearly understand the commander's commitment to equal opportunity. Commanders should also make the issue an agenda item when meeting with top advisors. This is done with other high-priority items and it reinforces the importance the commander places on the issue. In doing so, it raises the importance placed on it by others throughout the chain of command.

Navy leaders should also effectively evaluate the organizational climate of individual units. Individual units do not typically have personnel who are skilled in psychometrics or who are appropriately trained in designing other means of measuring organizational climates. Thus, appropriate instruments for measuring the climate should be provided and their use required. This will allow commanders to hear what personnel throughout the organization are saying about the organization's equal climate. Once they have heard, they should then act to remove barriers to equal opportunity.

Two of the most potent tools at the commander's discretion are the tools of rewards and discipline. Commanders send powerful statements each time they reward or punish personnel. Commanders who issue mild punishment to those found guilty of egregious discriminatory acts send the signal that such discriminatory acts are tolerated or that they are not serious. Similarly, commanders who issue awards that help sailors get promoted in spite of the fact that such sailors have been found guilty of discrimination, reinforce the culture of inequality. Thus, commanders must articulate their commitment to equality by both words and actions. However, if there is incongruence between words and actions, those in the organization are likely to hear the actions more loudly.

Revise the Current Evaluation System

In the Navy, evaluation reports are important for promotions at all levels. These evaluations are considered, along with other factors, at pay grades E-1 to E-7. In pay grades beyond E-7, those evaluations stand alone as overall depictions of sailors' performance. At the present, these evaluations represent little more than how the individual's supervisor says the service member has performed. These evaluations are purely subjective and little or no documentation is required to support the supervisor's assessment. Such high level of subjectivity leaves the evaluation reports very vulnerable to individual bias and favoritism. Participants in this study discuss how they believe rankings — which are a critical part of the evaluation report — were unjustly decided.

Because they are such an important part of the promotion process, the Navy must reduce the subjectivity of the evaluation process if it is to continue to move toward a more merit-based system. Supervisors should be required to retain documentation to support the evaluation remarks, scores, and rankings that are provided for each sailor under his or her authority. Moreover, when such remarks, scores, or rankings are challenged by the sailor, that sailor should be provided a hearing, at a level that is higher than the service member's supervisor, where justification for the remarks, scores, and ranking can be reviewed and a determination made. Such actions will increase the credibility of the evaluation system.

Eliminate the "Just Like Me" Factor

Another important factor that must be addressed is the tendency of supervisors and potential mentors to favor those who bear their skin color or who have a similar background. Although it is difficult to address, because it is such an important non-merit factor, the military cannot get to a meritocracy without addressing it. Sailors who are otherwise talented are being disadvantaged because of the way they walk or because of their manner of speaking or because of the type of music they like — all non-merit factors. Participants in this study discussed scenarios where sailors who worked for them were denied recognition based on these non-merit factors, in spite of how well these sailors performed. Moreover, some in the study discussed how decisions about mentor-protégé relationships were made based on these factors.

The decision to embrace racism or to be an agent for change is a very closely held and personal decision. However, to attempt to influence this decision, the Navy should direct its equal opportunity training in this area. Moreover, rather than only discuss equal opportunity as a Navy requirement and as the right thing to do, the service must also show how providing all sailors equal opportunities affects supervisors' performance of their duties and their careers and how it benefits the Navy.

However, in spite of its efforts, because military personnel are derived from an unjust society, there will likely be personnel who refuse to embrace the Navy's goal of creating a purely merit-based system. In these cases, the Navy must decide what type of organization it desires to be and whether it is willing to take the hard steps necessary to achieve that end. If it chooses meritocracy as its ultimate end, then it may be necessary to discharge those who refuse to embrace its objective. If the Navy really considers equal opportunity to be a true business imperative, then it must treat it as it would any other business imperative and rid itself of those who work against the organization's objectives.

Conclusion

The United States military has taken significant steps to create a more equal work environment for its service members and the services assert that they have created a purely merit-based system. They have written policies at different levels of the organization that prohibit discrimination based on certain factors and provide training for their personnel on issues relating to equal opportunity. Additionally, the Department of Defense created a Defense Equal Opportunity Management Institute to focus exclusively on educating the force on different aspects of equal opportunity. However, in spite of its efforts, some in the military services contend that the services continue to fall short of creating a work environment where merit is the sole determinant of success.

The Navy, as a component of the military, continues to show significant disparities between the achievement levels of African American men and their White counterparts. Moreover, African American men within the service contend that significant disparities exist between the opportunities afforded them and those afforded their White male colleagues in areas such as awards and recognition, job assignments, and evaluations. Moreover, while they agree that the Navy has probably exceeded the civilian sector in this area, those in this study unanimously disagree that the Navy has created an environment where merit alone determines one's level of success. They added that non-merit factors often play a significant role in determining outcomes and that African American men are often disadvantaged by these factors.

However, in spite of the disadvantages, some African American men do succeed and ascend to the highest enlisted ranks. To do this, they employ a number of coping mechanisms, including minimization, adaptation, overachieving, and self-definition. Moreover, while they feel they have endured negative experiences, the majority stated they did not retain negative feelings as a result of those experiences. Some used them as learning experiences and others simply viewed those barriers as challenges that they managed to overcome.

While these men managed to excel in spite of the barriers, many African American men do not. If the military is ever to achieve its stated goal of creating, within American society, an environment where merit is the sole determinant of success, then it must take concrete steps to eradicate the inequalities that are inherent in its system. The results of these inequalities are clearly evidenced in the services' own statistics and are borne witness to by the participants in this study.

References

Allen, T. (2006). "Faith Helps Edwards, Black Coaches Realize Dream as NFL Field Generals." Retrieved January 19, 2006, from www.blackathletesportsnetwork.net/artman/publish/printer_1450.shtml.

Andersson, F., Holzer, H. J., and Lane, J. I. (2005). *Moving Up or Moving On: Who Advances in the Low-Wage Labor Market?* New York: Russell Sage Foundation.

Baldwin, N. (1997, Winter). "Equal Promotional Opportunity in the United States Navy." *Journal of Political and Military Sociology*, vol. 25, pp. 187–209.

Beck, A. J., and Harrison, P. M. (2001). *Facts: Race, Prison, and the Drug Laws.* Washington, D.C.: U.S. Department of Justice.

Beck, A., and Mumola, C. J. (1999). *Prisoners in 1998.* Washington, D.C.: U.S. Department of Justice, Bureau of Justice Statistics.

Bell, E. L. (1990). "The Bicultural Life Experience of Career-Oriented Black Women." *Journal of Organizational Behavior*, 11 (2), 459–478.

Bell, J. (2005, March 7). "Group Seeks Diversity in NFL Front Offices." *USA Today Online.* Retrieved June 01, 2006, from Findarticles.com website: http://findarticles.com/p/articles/mi_kmusa/is_200503/ai_n13280410.

Besharov, D. J., Holzer, H. J., and Landry, B. (2005). *The Economic Stagnation of the Black Middle Class.* Washington, D.C.: U.S. Commission on Civil Rights.

Blank, R. and Schmidt, L. (2002). "Welfare, Work and Wages." In R. Blank and R. Haskins, eds. *The New World of Welfare* (p. 20). Washington, D.C: Brookings Institute.

Bogdan, R. C., and Biklen, S. K. (1982). *Qualitative Research for Education: An Introduction to Theory and Methods.* Boston: Allyn and Bacon.

Bouchard, T. (1995). "Breaking the Last Taboo." *Contemporary Psychology*, 40 (5).

Buckley, G. L. (2002). *American Patriots: The Story of Blacks in the Military from the Revolutionary War to Desert Storm.* New York: Random House.

Butler, R. (1999, Autumn). "Why Black Officers Fail." *Parameters*, pp. 54–69.

Calkins, C. (2004, January 15). "Defense Institute Gets New Home." *AFPN.* Retrieved June 07, 2006, from Findarticles.com website: http://findarticles.com/p/articles/mi_prfr/is_200401/ai_3913320385.

CNO (1999). *Inter-Deployment Training Cycle Workload Reduction Update.* Washington, D.C.: U.S. Department of Navy.

Cobbs, P. M. (2005). *My American Life: From Rage to Entitlement*. New York: Basic Books.
Cobbs, P. M., and Turnock, J. (2003). *Cracking the Corporate Code: The Revealing Success Stories of 32 African American Executives*. New York: Executive Leadership Council.
Cole, E., and Omari, S. (2003). "Race, Class and the Dilemmas of Upward Mobility for African Americans." *Journal of Social Issues*, 59 (4), 785–802.
Cole, E. R. (2005). "NFL Pioneer's Honor: Better Late than Never." Retrieved January 27, 2006, from http://www.IMDiversity.com.
Collins, S. M. (1983). "The Making of the Black Middle Class." *Social Problems*, 30, 369–382.
Cose, E. (2002). *The Envy of the World*. New York: Washington Square Press.
Crocker, J., and Major, B. (1989). "Social Stigma and Self-Esteem: The Self-Protective Properties of Stigma." *Psychological Review*, 96, 608–630.
Davidman, L. (2000). *Motherloss*. Berkeley: University of California Press.
Davis, J. A., and Smith, T. W. (1992). *The NORC General Social Survey: A User's Guide*. Newbury Park, CA: Sage.
Delaney, R. (2005). "African Americans in Motion Pictures." Long Island University. Retrieved February 9, 2006, from www.liu.edu/cwis/cwp/library/african/movies.htm.
Dirks, T. (2005). "Academy Awards: The Oscars." Retrieved February 3, 2006, from http://www.filmsite.org/oscars.html.
Dorfman, D. (1995). "Soft Science with a Neoconservative Agenda." *Contemporary Psychology*, 40 (5).
Du Bois, W. E. B. (1903; 1989) *The Souls of Black Folk*. New York: Bantam Books.
Duran, I. M. (2004). Remarks before Hispanic Association on Corporate Responsibility. Corporate Governance Conference, February 4, 2004, Washington, D.C.
Dworkin, R. (2000). *Sovereign Virtue*. Cambridge, MA: Harvard University Press.
Feagin, J. R., and Sikes, M. P. (1994). *Living with Racism: The Black Middle-Class Experience*. Boston: Beacon.
Feagin, J., Early, K., and McKinney, K. (2001). "Many Costs of Discrimination: The Case of Middle-Class African Americans." *Indiana Law Review*, 34, 1313–1360.
Fisher, C. S., Hout, C., Jaankowski, M. S., Lucas, S. R., Swidler, A., and Voss, K. (1996). *Inequality by Design: Cracking the Bell Curve Myth*. Princeton, NJ: Princeton University Press.
Garfinkel, H., and Sacks, H. (1970). "On Formal Structures of Practical Action." In J. C. McKinney and E. A. Tiryakin, eds. *Theoretical Sociology* (pp. 337–366). New York: Appleton-Century-Crofts.
Gettye, I. (1993, April). "Public Enemy Number One." *Afrique*, 4, 4.
Gilder, G. (1981). *Wealth and Poverty*. New York: Basic Books.
Gould, M. (1999). "Race and Theory: Culture, Poverty, and Adaptation to Discrimination." In J. Wilson and J. Ogbu, eds. *Sociological Theory* (pp.171–200). Malden, MA: Blackwell.
Groves, R. M., and Kahn, R. L. (1979). *Surveys by Telephone: A National Comparison with Personal Interviews*. New York: Academic Press.
Haney, C., and Zimbardo, P. (1998, July). "The Past and Future of U.S. Prison Policy: Twenty-Five Years after the Stanford Prison Experiment." *American Psychologist*, 53 (7).
Harrison, P., and Beck, A. (2005, October). *Bureau of Justice Statistics: Prisoners in 2004*. Washington, D.C.: U.S. Department of Justice.
Hendren, J. (2006, January 24). "Army Revises Death Penalty Rules." NPR Morning Edition. Washington, D.C.: National Public Radio.

Herrnstein, R., and Murray, C. (1994). *The Bell Curve: Intelligence and Class Structure in American Life*. New York: The Free Press.

Hill, J. (2006, January 22). "Coaching Still Black-and-White in NFL." Retrieved January 23, 2006, from http://nbowlsport.blogspot.com/2006/01/coaching-still-black-and-white-issue.html.

Hodge, J. (1995). *Black Women's Contributions*. Topical Research Internship Program. Patrick Air Force Base, FL: Defense Equal Opportunity Management Institute.

Hoepfl, M. C. (1997, Fall). "Choosing Qualitative Research: A Primer for Technology Education Researchers." *Journal of Technology*, 9, 1.

Holohan, C. J., Moos, R. H., and Schaefer, J. A. (1996). "Coping, Stress Resistance, and Growth: Conceptualizing Adaptive Functioning." In M. Zeidner and N. S. Endler, eds. *Handbook of Coping* (pp. 24–43). New York: John Wiley and Sons.

Huber, J., and Form, W. (1973). *Income and Ideology: An Analysis of the American Political Formula*. New York: Free Press.

Hutchinson, E. O. (2002). "Blacks Still Losing Race to Corporate Top." Retrieved June 01, 2006, from http://www.alternet.org/columnists/story/12364.

Johnson, J. B. (2005, February 10). "Black CEOs Gaining in Corporate America. Numbers Growing: 18 Join Magazine's List of Top Execs." Retrieved July 01, 2006, from *San Francisco Chronicle Online*, website http://www.sfgate.com/cgi-bin/article.cgi?file=/chronicle/archive/2005/02/10/BUGDRB8K781.DTLandtype=business.

Johnson, R. S. (2006). "Blackout of '06: Despite On-Field Success, Coaching Vacancies Aren't Going to Black Coaches." AOL Black Voices. Retrieved July 30, 2006, from http://blackvoices.aol.com/black_sports/special/_a/blackout-of-06/20060123121909990010.

King, G., Keohane, R.O., and Verba, S. (1994). *Designing Social Inquiry: Scientific Inference in Qualitative Research*. Princeton, NJ: Princeton University Press.

Kanazawa, M. T., and Funk, J. P. (2001, October). "Racial Discrimination in Professional Basketball: Evidence from Nielsen Ratings." *Economic Inquiry*, 39, 4.

Kotter, J., and Heskett, J. (1992). *Corporate culture and performance*. New York: The Free Press.

Kram, K. E. (1985). *Mentoring at Work: Developmental Relationships in Organizational Life*. Glenview, IL: Scott Foresman.

Ladd, E. (1994). *The American Ideology*. Storrs, CT: The Roper Center for Public Opinion Research.

Lavrakas, P.J. (1993). *Telephone Survey Methods: Sampling, Selection, and Supervision*. 2d ed. Newbury Park, CA: Sage.

Lee, J. (2000). "The Salience of Race in Everyday Life: Black Customers' Shopping Experience in Black and White Neighborhoods." *Work and Occupations*, 27, 353–376.

Major, B., Richards, M. C., Cooper, M. L., Cozzarelli, C., and Zubek, J. (1998). "Personal Resilience, Cognitive Appraisals, and Coping: An Integrative Model of Adjustment to Abortion." *Journal of Personality and Social Psychology*, 74, 735–752.

Marshall, C., and Rossman, G. B. (1999). *Designing Qualitative Research*. 3d ed. Thousand Oaks, CA: Sage.

McNamee, S., and Miller, R. K. (2004, Spring). "The Meritocracy Myth." *Sociation Today*, 2 (1).

Meierhoefer, B. S. (1992). *The General Effect of Mandatory Minimum Prison Terms: A Longitudinal Study of Federal Sentences Imposed*. Washington, D.C.: Federal Judicial Center.

Miller, C. T., and Kaiser, C. R. (2001). "Implications of Mental Models of Self and Others for the Targets of Stigmatization." In M. R. Leary, ed. *Interpersonal Rejection* (pp. 189–212). New York: Oxford University Press.

Mirowsky, J., and Ross, C. E. (1989). *Social Causes of Psychological Distress*. New York: Aldine de Gruyter.

Moen, P., Dempster-McClain, D., and Walker, H. A. (1999). *A Nation Divided: Diversity, Inequality and Community in American Society*. London: Cornell University Press.

Morgan, G. (1997). *Images of Organization*. Thousand Oaks, CA: Sage.

Moss, A. A. (1994). *From Slavery to Freedom*. New York: McGraw Hill.

Moynihan, D. (1965). *The Negro Family: The Case for National Action*. Washington, D.C.: Office of Policy Planning and Research, U.S. Department of Labor.

Mumford, D. M., Marks, M. M., Connelly, M. S., Zacaro, S.J., and Reitner-Palmon, R. (2000). "Development of Leadership Skills: Experience and Timing." *Leadership Quarterly*, 11, 87–114.

Navy Core Values. Navy Personnel Development. Retrieved October 01, 2006, from http://www.Navy.com/about/during/personaldevelopment/honor.

Neckerman, K. M., Carter, P., and Lee, J. (1999). "Segmented Assimilation and Minority Cultures of Mobility." *Ethnic and Racial Studies*, 22, 945–965.

Neuman, W. L. (2003). *Social Research Methods: Qualitative and Quantitative Approaches*. Boston: Allyn and Bacon.

"Oath of Enlistment." (n.d.). Wikipedia, the free encyclopedia. Retrieved October 01, 2006, from Reference.com website: http://www.reference.com/browse/wiki/Oath_of_enlistment.

Pager, D. (2003). "The Mark of a Criminal Record." *American Sociological Review*, 67(4), 526–546.

Peshkin, A. (1993). "The Goodness of Qualitative Research." *Educational Researcher*, 22(2), 23–29.

Polkinghorne, D. (1983). *Methodology for the Human Sciences*. Albany: State University of New York Press.

Quester, A., and Gilroy, C. (2002, April). "Women and Minorities in America's Volunteer Military." *Contemporary Economic Policy*, 20 (2), 111–121.

Reutter, M. (2000, August). "Top Male, Female Pay in Like Jobs Comparable, but Few Women Run." *News Bureau*, University of Illinois at Urbana-Champaign.

Rudner, R. S. (1966). *Philosophy of Science*. Englewood Cliffs, NJ: Prentice Hall.

Ruggiero, K. M., Taylor, D. M., and Lydon, J. E. (1997). "How Disadvantaged Group Members Cope with Discrimination When They Perceive That Social Support is Available." *Journal of Applied Social Psychology*, 27, 1581–1600.

Scarville, J., Scott, B. B., Edwards, J., Lancaster, A., and Elig, T.W. (1999). *Armed Forces Equal Opportunity Survey*. Arlington, VA: Defense Manpower Data Center.

Scheffler, S. (2003, Winter). "What is Egalitarianism?" *Philosophy and Public Affairs*, 1, 5–39.

Schneider, W. (1997). *Developing Organizational Consultancy*. New York: Routledge.

Shapiro, T. M. (2004). *Assets for Change*. Waltham, MA: Heller School for Social Policy and Management, Brandeis University.

Singleton, R. A., and Straits, B. C. (1999). *Approaches to Social Research*. New York: Oxford University Press.

Slaght, K. (2003). Mentor program. *SPAWAR INSTRUCTION 1734.1*. San Diego, CA: Department of the Navy.

Steele, S. (1990). *The Content of Our Character*. New York: St. Martin's Press.

Strauss, A., and Corbin, J. (1990). *Basics of Qualitative Research: Grounded Theory Procedures and Techniques*. Newbury Park, CA: Sage.
Swanson, C. B. (2003). *Who Graduates? Who Doesn't?* Washington, D.C: The Urban Institute, Education Policy Center.
Trower, C. A., and Chait, R. P. (2002, March–April). "Faculty Diversity." *Harvard Magazine*. Retrieved March 10, 2006, from http://www.harvardmagazine.com/on-line/030218.html.
Uniform Code of Military Justice. (n.d.). Wikipedia, the free encyclopedia. Retrieved October 01, 2006, from Reference.com website: http://www.reference.com/browse/wiki/Uniform_Code_of_Military_Justice.
U.S. Coast Guard (2005). *FY06 Lieutenant Commander Selection and Lieutenant Continuation Boards*. Arlington, VA: Department of Homeland Security.
U.S. Congress, Committee on Armed Forces (1973). *Racial Incidents onboard USS* Kitty Hawk *(CVA-63) and USS* Constellation *(CVA-64) in 1972*. Washington, D.C.: Government Printing Office.
U.S. Equal Employment Opportunity Commission (2005). *2005 Performance and Accountability Report*. Washington, D.C.: U.S. Equal Employment Opportunity Commission.
U.S. Marine Corps (2005). *FY04 Profile of Marine Corps*. Washington, D.C.: Department of the Navy.
U.S. Navy (2001b). *Navy Equal Opportunity Policy*. Washington, D.C.: Department of the Navy.
U.S. Navy (2001a). *Advancement Manual for the Advancement of Enlisted Personnel of the U.S. Navy and U.S. Naval Reserve*. Millington, TN: Department of the Navy.
U.S. Navy (2006). *Navy-Wide Demographic Data for First Quarter FY 2006*. Millington, TN: Department of the Navy.
U.S. Navy (2005). *Navy-Wide Demographic Data for Fourth Quarter FY 2005*. Millington, TN: Department of the Navy.
Vanneman, R., and Cannon, L. W. (1987). *The American Perception of Class*. Philadelphia: Temple University Press.
Verdieu, G. (2004, December 2). "Marxism and the Right to Self-Determination." *Workers World News*, p. 1.
Walter, J. C. (1996). "The Changing Status of the Black Athlete in the 20th Century United States." Retrieved July 28, 2006, from http://www.americansc.org.uk/Online/walters.htm.
Welch, R., and Angulo, C.T. (2000). *Justice on Trial: Racial Disparities in the American Criminal Justice System*. Washington, D.C.: Leadership Conference on Civil Rights.
Wengraf, T. (2001). *Qualitative Research Interviewing*. Thousand Oaks, CA: Sage.
Whited, F. (2006). "Black Head Coaches: History vs. Reality." Retrieved July 28, 2006, from http://www.blackathlete.net/artman/publish/article_01451.shtml.
Wilson, W. J. (1996). *When Work Disappears*. New York: Vintage Books.

Index

Acceptance 92–93, 105
Adaptation 143–145
Advancement Manual 15, 23
Affirmative action 101, 118–120
African American men: coping 16–19; discharge statistics 12; discipline statistics 3–4; promotion statistics 4–5, 9–10
African American women 13
Allen, T. 108
Anti-discrimination policies 131
Assimilation 17, 80, 93, 116
Assignments 154–155
Attainment levels 5
Awards 42, 133–134, 149

Baldwin, N. 12
Barriers to inclusion 30, 37, 55–56, 63–66, 72–73, 82–83, 95–97, 108–122
Battle of Bunker Hill 7
Behavioral conditioning 21
Bell, Ella 17

Cannon, L.W. 18
Carter, P. 18
Caulkins, C. 11
Changing to fit in 79–80
Climate assessments 163
Coast Guard 9
Cobbs, Price 18
Cole, E. 18, 141
Collins, S.M. 18
Competence questioned 153
Congressional Hispanic Caucus Institute 15
Cooper, M.L. 19

Coping strategies 17, 139–151
Cose, Ellis 3, 17
Cozzarelli, C. 19
Crocker, J. 18, 141

Defense Equal Opportunity Management Institute 11, 157, 161
Defense Race Relations Institute 157
Disparity in views of navy equal opportunity 8–9
Diversity training 71, 138
DuBois, W.E.B. 17
Duran, Ingrid 15

Equal Opportunity Survey 8
Evaluation system 165
Exceptional Negro 115–116

Feagin, J.R. 17, 160
Fitting in 31–32, 69, 79, 93, 112

Gilroy, C. 11
Good ol' boys club 73, 109
Great Lakes, IL 21

Hallock, Kevin 13
Heskett, J. 111
Hill, J. 108
Hispanic Association on Corporate Responsibility 15
Hispanic underrepresentation 15
Hodge, J. 13
Holohan, C.J. 19

In-group/out-group dynamics 111, 154–156

USS *Ingleside* 86
Integration 47, 71, 81, 94, 106, 135

Just like me factor 165

Kaiser, C.R. 18
USS *Kitty Hawk* 11
Kotter, J. 111
Kram, K.E. 123, 128
Ku Klux Klan 56

Leadership 164
Lee, J. 18
Lydon, J.E. 19

Major, B. 18, 19, 141
Marine Corps 5, 9–10
Mentorship 25, 30, 43–45, 52, 58–60, 67–68, 77, 89–90, 102–103, 123–129
Meritocracy 7, 10, 47–48, 53–54, 60, 70–71, 80–81, 105–106, 130–138, 157
Military code 20–21
Military training 21–22
Miller, C.T. 18
Minimization 18, 145
Minority culture of mobility 18
Minority status 146
Mirowsky, J. 18, 141, 146, 148, 158, 160
Moos, R.H. 19
Morgan, G. 16–17
Mumford, D.M. 123, 126

Navy Equal Opportunity & Sexual Harassment Survey 12
Navy selection boards 23
Navy technical schools 110–111
Neckerman, K.M. 18
Negative feelings 50–51, 56–57, 75, 86, 160
Non-judicial punishment 10

Oath of Enlistment 20
Omari, S. 18, 141
Organizational Culture 112
Overachieving 142–143

Participants' profiles 28–107
Perceptions of equal opportunity 8
Policy statements 162, 164
Promotion process 22–25, 46, 48, 49–50

Quester, A. 11
Questioning Competence 116–118

Race as a positive factor 33, 45, 79, 118
Racial jokes and epithets 78–79, 87, 121–122
Reassess current state 162
Resilience 139
Reverse discrimination 120, 155
Revolutionary War 8
Richards, M.C. 19
Robinson, Brenda 13
Role models 120–122, 156–157
Ross, C.E. 18, 141, 146, 148, 158, 160
Ruggiero, K.M. 19, 145

Scarville, J. 9
Schaefer, J.A. 19
Schneider, W. 12
Self-Definition 147–151
Sikes, M.P. 17, 160
Slaught, K. 26
Social avoidance 18
Social exclusion 19, 37–38
Specialized training 155

Taylor, D.M. 19
Theus, Lucius 11
Tokenism 70, 115–116

Uniform Code of Military Justice 20
United States Navy Regulations 20

Vanneman, R. 18
Vietnam War 10–11

White sailors 68, 89–90, 103–104, 136–137

Zubek, J. 19

www.ingramcontent.com/pod-product-compliance
Lightning Source LLC
Chambersburg PA
CBHW021914180426
43198CB00035B/579